WAS IT BECAUSE I SWALLOWED?
A Cautionary Tale of a
Groupie Turned Celebrity Braider
Chasing Paper in the ATL

CELESTE DUARTE

Photo By Warren Cameron—5acresstudio.com

Hair by Terina "Tee" Meekins

Cover design by Octavis Anderson ll, Graphic Designer
F3 Media ll Atlanta, Georgia
Website: http://f3mediawork.wix.com/f3media ll bubbyosa.tumblr.com

Almost instantly the title probably suggests that this book isn't going to be socially responsible, but trust me: it is. Whether we choose to admit it or not, we are all guilty of swallowing our emotions in one form or another: pride or guilt, hurt or loss, shame or insecurity, the truth, or someone else's lies. I have swallowed way more emotions than the average person should be allowed, but in the midst of it all, I found my foundation and its words and me, so here they are.

Acknowledgments

I am thankful to God for his grace, which allowed me to connect the dots and make sense of it all.

To my brother Jeffrey, whose spirit has lived within me since the day he crossed over. I love you.

To my mummy, I love you!

To my daddy, whose words of wisdom helped to carry me through many what I'd considered dark days.

To the only sister God gave me, I wouldn't trade you for the world. I love you!

To my cousin Pooh for not believing some of my stories and making me take pictures and mail them as proof. Thanks for encouraging me to keep it moving when the circumstances were out of my control.

To the best friend any person could ever have, Tonya from Los Angeles, who probably remembers almost every story just as vividly as I do. Her listening skills were on point and span over two decades. Tonya, to you and yours, I love you!

To all my family including my extended family who love me unconditionally, thanks for believing in me. Thank you to Tony M., Venessa, Meka, my godsister Sabrina, Desol, the Howard family, Phatboy, Mike, Brandy, and Tracie.

To Mr. Igbo, you could be on another planet, and I would still figure a way to come see about you.

I also wish to thank the whole Old Fourth Ward neighborhood for feeding me over the years, especially Caramba Restaurant, Red, Amy, Thad, and Stacy B. Thank you, too, to my neighbor Yatrea.

I have a special thanks to my postal lady, Nezzie, for cheering me on at the mailbox. To my realtor, Ms. Rita, who worked for pennies on the dollar, I got you because hard work never goes unnoticed. Thanks are also in order for Chris Hunt of Hunt Brothers Tinting and the Patrick family, both out of Decatur, Georgia. Thank you to YourVitaminLady Herb Shop on Auburn Avenue.

Even if I forgot to mention you, thanks for helping me to hold it down. I love you guys.

CHAPTER 1

The year was 2006. My shit was fucked up, and I was facing foreclosure on my Atlanta condominium. It was my first home, and it sat just one block away from the historic birth home of Dr. Martin Luther King Jr. My homeowner's association pursued me as if I was an outlaw for past-due fees; my uninsured Mercedes ML 320 had expired tags, and the car repo man was on the prowl. Worst of all, I couldn't even feed my dog, Lucky, my loyal companion of nine years. I was forced to give him away, which ultimately cost him his life. I didn't know how this could possibly be happening to me: I had friends who were millionaires, pro athletes, and celebrities. I knew they wouldn't let me go out like that.

But I'm getting way ahead of myself. Let me start from the beginning.

The year was 1986, and I was eighteen. I looked down from the second-story studio apartment's horizontal window, which spanned the entire length of the room and made it easy for me to see every move on the two-lane street outside. In what seemed like slow motion, two plainclothes police officers jumped out of their dark, unmarked vehicle and ran toward the apartment building. Before I knew it, they were on the stairwell and would be banging on the cast-iron gate at any moment. For some reason this didn't strike me as a standard drug raid, so I wasn't afraid of the outcome. Instead, I said, "Fuck it," took the plastic freezer bag filled with quarter bags of prepackaged crack, and hid them. I flushed the toilet a couple of times, pretending to dispose of the evidence, and taped the bag underneath one of the drawers adjacent to the bathroom sink. I ran from the bathroom to the front door as if I had no idea what was going on. I yelled out to sleepyhead, whose name I couldn't remember because I'd met him only the day before, "Police!"

He was asleep on the sofa, totally oblivious to what was going on. That's when the police began to shout, "Police! Open up!" They hit the gate with an unknown object and demanded that we open the front door. I threw open the gate and let them in.

"Hands above your head!" one of the officers yelled. "Get up, and get over here!" he said to the young black guy in the apartment with me.

The first officer questioned us while the second began to ransack the apartment, flinging open all the kitchen cabinets and drawers, obviously looking for narcotics or cash or both. I just knew he was gonna check the bathroom as well and find my secret stash. These cops must've had some inside information that led them to this apartment. In the back of my mind, I kept asking, "Where is the rest of this DEA task force?" These punk-ass officers mentioned nothing about a warrant even when I finally allowed them entry into the apartment. As a matter of fact, I never heard any sirens going off, either. It didn't matter. I felt confident that I had a story that would work to get me out of this situation. I'd been hanging out in that same apartment long enough with the Jamaican guy who actually lived there to know there was no back door to escape from, so I had no choice but to bullshit my way out.

The first officer came at me with all kinds of questions. "What are your names?" he asked, demanding an answer from the both of us.

With my thick New England accent that I consider worse than a New Yorker's, I said, "Celeste." I said that I had just moved to Los Angeles last week, when in fact I'd been living there for almost a year. I pretended that I had no idea why this was happening as I watched the second officer and his every move. I told the first officer that I had gotten a ride from some guy who had just dropped me off at this apartment and promised to come back for me shortly. As far as I was concerned, it was still daylight outside, and I didn't see anything wrong with waiting for my ride to come back and get me as an excuse for being there in the first place.

I guess the officer was satisfied with my story because he turned away from me and began interrogating the other guy with the same line of questioning. Ole boy was about seventeen, fair skinned, five foot seven, no more than 150 pounds soaking wet, and badly in need of barbershop attention. He said that he was couch-hopping and kinda homeless and just catching up on some sleep. He began to explain that he thought this was his homeboy's cousin's apartment and that his homeboy had promised to come back to get him as well.

The second officer shouted, "Well, who flushed the toilet?"

As politely as I knew how, I said, "I just used the restroom, sir."

It seemed both officers realized they had no reason to charge us for anything, so they let us go and told us not to come back. Had they seen the shotgun behind the door they had pulled closed on their way out, they may have changed their minds.

As the teenager and I gleefully walked downstairs and away from the four-unit complex, he asked me what happened to the goods.

"Told you. I flushed them down the toilet," I said, trusting that word would get back to the Jamaican and I would be free and in the clear. After the boy and I separated, I waited about fifteen minutes before I ran back upstairs to get the goods. I brought them back to my apartment just a few miles away and handed them to my boyfriend, who knew absolutely nothing about being a drug dealer or how to unload the $2,000 worth of crack I'd just handed to him.

The previous year I had relocated from Providence, Rhode Island, to Los Angeles. I was staying with my dad's sister, who had taken me in shortly after I'd graduated from high school. Being born and raised in Providence wasn't such a bad thing as far as I can remember. My mom and dad split when I was a toddler, and my aunties, uncles, great-aunts, great-uncles, and cousins—some of whom weren't too much older than I was—were always watching out for us kids and seemed to dictate our every move. My older brother and sister, my little brother, and I were never alone. If family wasn't visiting our apartment, then friends of the family were. Both my mom's and dad's grandparents were from Brava, Cape Verde. My dad's mother once spoke only Portuguese; she was forced to learn English in order to communicate with her kids. The Cape Verde Islands sit just off the west coast of Africa and are centered between Portugal and Africa. However, my mother has always told me to put African American as my nationality because we identified with that race more than any other.

At an early age, I could see that my mom had it hard trying to make ends meet. That alone made me want to earn some form of income for her and myself. I was so eager to earn cash that at twelve years old, I joined an agency called Call-A-Teen and did odd jobs like washing apartment walls at senior assisted-living centers. On plenty of weekends, I would wash glasses and ashtrays, wipe down tables, and sweep and mop for one of my mom's cousins who ran an after-hours spot. I even babysat for the young mothers on my block. At times it seemed I was running a day care, I'd be watching so many kids. If there was any way to make money, I would find it.

In New England at any early age, from May until September—when the weather was good—I tried to stay outside and play kick the can or hide-and-seek with the neighborhood kids. When the weather got really cold, I stayed upstairs in my room with my endless girlfriends and cousins, playing dolls. All in all, I was a good kid who got decent grades in school and barely got in trouble with teachers. That's only because I was always trying to stay on my mom's good side. Like some Portuguese women, my mother constantly yelled, sometimes for no reason at all.

I was a late bloomer and played with Barbie dolls until I was fourteen. But when I turned fifteen, my hourglass shape, pretty face, and silky, semilong hair began attracting the attention of grown men, which let me know that I could put down the dolls and play with the real boys instead.

The more I grew, the more attention I got from boys and men. The more attention I received, the more my family and extended family became protective of me. I couldn't walk anywhere without having to beat boys off with a stick. I began to like the attention and sometimes flirted back. Soon I had boyfriends on the east, west, north, and south sides of town. My family didn't like it. In their eyes I was still a kid.

At sixteen, even though I was still a virgin, my body was so fierce that my elders assumed I was having sex. If I was spotted out somewhere by an auntie, uncle, or even a distant cousin, they'd investigate. The questions would hail around me like gunfire: "Who is this guy you're with? Who is his family? What do you have on? What are you doing with those people?"

This was the norm for me till I turned eighteen.

I know now that my family was only trying to protect me. But back then their concern was irritating. It prompted me to flee from the East Coast to the West.

As soon as I arrived in California, I moved in with my auntie and her four young daughters in the Monterey Park area of Los Angeles. Within six months I'd already witnessed various lifestyles of the rich and famous while driving along the Pacific Coast Highway and through areas like Beverly Hills and Bel Air. Luxurious lifestyles were no longer just on television like when I was a little girl. I always wanted to have money because I thought it would make life easier. I knew I couldn't get rich overnight, especially since I had no clue as to how I would even start trying to get paid. So I got a job as a receptionist to pay for bills and my own apartment and decided to just enjoy California living until something came to me.

I met my future boyfriend and the man I thought was the love of my life not long after getting my first place. Lawrence was nineteen and had skin the color of brown sugar. He was about five foot eleven and around 190 pounds, with silky Indian hair. He and I met at the Carolina West, a club on Century Boulevard near the Los Angeles airport.

The moment I laid eyes on him, I was smitten. It was dark inside the club, but he appeared to glow as he stood alone next to the dance floor. I wanted to get his attention but just didn't know how, so I pushed him down the four steps that led to the dance floor. As I held out my hand to help him up, I confessed over the loud music that the push had been intentional. I didn't know what else to do; at that moment all I wanted was to step out of my panties and wrap my thighs around his head. He was so beautiful that I was already thinking about how attractive our kids would be. He was funny and open-minded, and did I say gorgeous?

Immediately we began living together. In six months, we were almost dressing alike and were inseparable. We enjoyed each other so much that we didn't care about the rest of the world. We stayed in the house as much as we could, and although I was still immature when it came to sex, we had more sex than I'd ever had with any man. After sex we'd have plenty of pillow talk. In those conversations, we planned to get married and grow old together. We even scheduled a future visit to see his mother, who was living in Denver, Colorado at the time.

Things were really moving along nicely for us, and I was falling hard. I loved everything about him. But every now and then, he would show signs of jealousy, which made me really uncomfortable.

At the time, I worked part-time as a hostess for a local black-owned restaurant. Out of nowhere, Lawrence started commenting on my outfits: he said they were too fitted. I told him there wasn't much I could do about it—I had to wear the black pants and shirt I had on because that was the restaurant's standard. He seemed to accept that, and I overlooked the fact that this man thought he should tell me how I should dress in order to make my money.

Actually, I thought it was cute that he took such an interest in how I dressed. On my days off, he would dictate what I could and couldn't wear outside the house. When I think about it now, I see that wasn't normal behavior, but I kept telling myself that the longer we were together, the more he would trust me. That didn't happen.

Two months into our relationship, Lawrence thought that I was fucking around on him. We lived in Inglewood at the time. All the apartments had entrances on the same side of the building—no back doors—so the point of entry and exit could easily be seen from across the street. They looked just like the apartments in the movie *Baby Boy* that Tyrese's baby momma, Taraji Henson, stayed in.

One morning Lawrence had stationed himself across the street behind some bushes. A coworker from the restaurant where I worked came by unannounced and was there for just ten minutes to drop something off. After he left, I closed the door and went back to watching TV. Lawrence suddenly busted through the door, walked across the living room, and—without saying a word— hauled off and punched me in my eye. He had obviously momentarily gone mad and thought some kind of sex had gone down. I was so shocked and hurt, I forgot to cry.

Later that evening Lawrence promised nothing like that would never happen again. My eye was black-and-blue for a week, but I dismissed it because I thought he loved me.

As a child, I'd watched my mother's ex-husband beat her down almost regularly. They constantly had altercations, especially when they got drunk. My older brother, sister, and I would jump in the fight to help my mom, grabbing everything from frying pans to broomsticks to vases to help beat the man off her. As an adult, I never bothered to ask my mother much about that stuff because it had happened so long ago. But I promised myself I wasn't going to be a victim of domestic violence.

After that first assault, my relationship with Lawrence coasted along until his arrest for drug-related offenses in 1987, not too long after I'd handed him that bag of crack. I wasn't there when it happened, but apparently he was caught red-handed with crack in his possession. A chase ensued, and one of the cops took aim and shot him in the ass. In addition to the drug charges, he was charged with assault of a peace officer and assault of civilians because he had pistol-whipped several people shortly before being pursued by the police.

While he was incarcerated, to prove my love for him, I got his name tattooed on my arm. I felt it was partly my fault that he was in prison in the first place, so I was gonna ride or die for him.

I know it sounds crazy, but—understand—I had never experienced love the way Lawrence loved me, and I wasn't ready to walk away from him. Maybe it was the way he looked me in my eyes when he'd tell me how much he loved me. I don't know.

For the first year and a half, I followed him from county jail to county jail, to a youth detention center, and to his final destination at California Correctional Institute at Tehachapi. The first few months in Los Angeles County were the hardest because I didn't have a car and had to take the bus to the downtown area of Los Angeles near skid row just to visit him. Our visits were special. I made sure there was always money on his books, and he would tell me how much he loved me, needed me, and couldn't live without me. That was all I needed to hear in order to stay dog-devoted to him.

Shortly after his sentencing, he was sent up to California State Prison Tehachapi, not far from Bakersfield. During one of my visits to Tehachapi, Lawrence and I were having a conversation when he casually asked, "So, you wanna get married so we can have conjugal visits?"

I didn't skip a beat. "Hell yeah," I replied. It was that simple. Nothing spectacular. I applied for our marriage certificate, and within months the prison chaplain performed our wedding ceremony. I didn't care how we did; it I just wanted to continue to be able to have sex with the man I loved.

On the drive back through the Mojave Desert, I told myself that our marriage would have to be on the sly. I wouldn't tell a single soul besides my closest friends, Tonya and Tracie.

In the winter of 1992, after four years, Lawrence was released, and we resumed right where we had left off. Even though financially we were OK because I had been working as an administrative assistant while Lawrence was locked up, our marriage was beginning to fall apart.

It seemed Lawrence had learned nothing in prison except how to perfect the drug game. After he was released, he jumped right back in the fray as if he hadn't missed a beat. Even after he'd been out for months, Lawrence wasn't doing anything but working on his second strike with the California penal system by associating with his newfound ex-convict friends. Lawrence was flashier than ever with his expensive Versace clothes, jewelry, new rims, and vogue tires. It was almost as if he'd learned how to be a real criminal while he was locked up, when before he was just playing.

I was conflicted as hell. I didn't want him dealing with those clowns he was running with, but he was yanking down that Hollywood loot I'd always fantasized about. With that money, he bought me a three-carat diamond ring, multiple single-carat rings, big gold earrings—three different sizes for all the holes in my ears—and a white miniature poodle. I was starting to enjoy the life we were living, but as I feared, Lawrence got sloppy, and a probation violation led him back to prison.

In all the years that Lawrence and I were together, I never cheated on his ass. Too bad I found out that he was consistently unfaithful to me shortly after he hit the streets.

I discovered he had two other girlfriends: one he called his bitch. These women apparently accepted the knowledge of each other, and me as his wife.

The one Lawrence referred to as his bitch gave birth to a baby girl. The baby was six months old when I found out about her little ass.

If I hadn't stopped by my ex-in-law's house one day and seen a baby there who was the spitting image of my husband, I may never have known. I felt betrayed because I wanted to wait to have his children but believed we were too young to start a family.

That night when I got home, I searched for clues in my husband's dresser drawers—pictures or even paperwork in another female's name—something to prove he may have fathered this baby. But I didn't find shit. I was fed up, especially when he never made it home that night.

The next morning, I woke up to find him asleep in a chair in front of the TV. I hurried back to the bedroom, grabbed his pistol, and pressed the front of the barrel to his lips.

He woke up, and his eyes got all big when he saw the gun damn near in his mouth and me standing behind it, shaking and looking crazy. I told him to admit the baby was his, and that he better not try to fucking lie about it.

I couldn't believe it, but Lawrence laughed. Moments later he admitted the baby was indeed his, as if it was no big deal.

Getting the info I was looking for, I put the gun down and prepared to get the beat down I knew was coming. He pushed me to the floor, got on top of me, smacked me across the face a couple of times, and then began choking me, saying I better not ever do that shit again.

Even though I promised I wouldn't be a victim like my mom, I began to lose count of the senseless fights I endured at the hands of Lawrence.

I finally accepted that we were both too young for marriage. I couldn't handle it. I knew I had to get away from him.

When he got locked up again for a second probation violation, I moved out immediately. I took everything—our contemporary furnishings, the floor-model television, even our waterbed mattress—leaving nothing but the lint on the carpet.

I began to move on with my life without him, but Lawrence couldn't handle it. When he got out, he told my girls to tell me that if he ever found me, I'd be sorry. The straw that broke the camel's back was when he ran up on me out with another man.

I was having dinner at a popular seafood spot in the marina with a guy I had met only days earlier. Lawrence came over to our table, shouted that I was his wife, and then threatened to beat my date down. He continued to shout, claiming that he would beat not only my current date, but any man he caught me with. That moment I realized that I'd swallowed enough of his abuse and didn't need to see any more. I had to get the hell out of LA. I was smart, outgoing, and only in my twenties. I had always told myself I could do anything I wanted to in life. It was time to stop saying it and start doing it.

CHAPTER 2

My cousin Minga had recently moved back to Richmond, Virginia, from Los Angeles, so I decided to call her to see if she could use a roommate. Lucky for me, she could.

Minga was my daddy's first cousin's daughter. She was six years older than I was but resembled me a great deal. She was petite and light skinned with an hourglass shape just like mine but not as thick.

I arrived at Minga's two-bedroom, two-bathroom apartment in midsummer 1994. It was a fairly new complex, only a couple of miles from Richmond International Airport and just minutes from downtown Richmond. Other than the sound of planes taking off and landing all day, everything about the location seemed a good fit for me.

I knew I could easily find work to make ends meet, but I wasn't exactly sure about applying to college. It was a good thing that I'd already visited Virginia Union University, a historically black college that my auntie and her girlfriends had attended a decade earlier. I'd visited Richmond and that very same campus while they were students in the early eighties.

Determined as hell to make a go of my recent move, one week after applying, I went to the admissions office and demanded to speak with the director, who told me I'd already been accepted. I was ecstatic.

The city of Richmond seemed much more laid-back than Los Angeles. By that fall I was taking my math and English prerequisite courses. I was happy to be doing something productive. School gave me a reason for being there; otherwise, the city was really boring. I managed to find a part-time gig with American Airlines as a ticket agent. That helped me manage my finances that first year. Even more rewarding was knowing that I'd be the first of my mom's kids to earn a college degree.

The following year, as a reward to myself for finishing my freshman year with honors, I flew back to Los Angeles for a few weeks. I returned to Inglewood in July 1995 and comfortably jumped back into the mix as if I'd never left. I began making my usual visits to see my family and friends and to eat at my favorite restaurants. After a week or so, I hooked up with one of my old hair stylists and homegirls, Sheila. She was a big-boned, dark-skinned chick who was built like SpongeBob, but super cool.

In conversation Sheila mentioned the upcoming Mike Tyson fight. She said Mike would be fighting Peter McNeeley the following weekend in Las Vegas and that she and another friend, Asia, were thinking of driving the three and a half hours to the festivities. Sheila asked if I'd be interested in going because they needed another person to split the expenses. Without hesitation I said, "I'm down!"

The following weekend Sheila picked me up in her compact car, and I was introduced to Asia. Asia appeared to be a mix of black and Asian, with a real pretty face, short, shiny jet-black hair, a small waist, and a big butt just like mine.

During our ride to Las Vegas, we boasted about how much fun we would have and all the men we would hook up with.

The ride went real smooth and seemed to take less time than I thought it would. We pulled up to the Hard Rock Casino. It had a huge fluorescent guitar out front that made me even more excited. After checking in to the casino, I overheard Asia say she would be meeting up later with some other friends of hers. I was thinking, "What happened to splitting the room three ways? And where were those additional chicks when it was time to check in to our room?" I knew something was wrong, but I thought, "Fuck it! I'm not going to let that ruin my fun."

I put my bags up in our room, put on my swimsuit, and headed to the pool to relax. Asia had dropped her bags off to go meet up with some Miami Heat NBA player. After a couple of hours of relaxation by the Hard Rock sandy pool, I returned to our room to find our new roommates. I pretended to be surprised as Asia introduced them. They claimed to be associates of Death Row Records, but I just kept wondering where their share of the room rent was.

The leader of the pack called herself Diamond. Diamond was a brown-skinned, thick female. She was about five foot three or so and somewhat attractive. She wore heavy makeup and hair extensions. I had already recognized one of the other females from Tupac's "To Live and Die in LA" video. Michelle was her name, but everyone called her Chelle. She was the driver of the old-school convertible in Tupac's video. Chelle was also brown-skinned, a bit over five feet, and only kinda cute.

The other two females were just OK looking and didn't say much, just laughed at anything remotely funny that anyone said.

While we all chatted, out of nowhere Diamond started singing a verse from Snoop Dogg's "Gin and Juice" and then one from Dr. Dre's "Let Me Ride," and immediately I recognized her voice. I no longer had any doubt about her Death Row affiliation.

I was like, "Enough idle chat. I'm ready to hit the casinos." So I jumped in the shower and got dressed only to wait for everyone else to get ready. Finally, when Asia exited the bathroom, the girls were more ready than I was to go.

We hit the MGM Grand Casino lobby seven deep and were getting all the attention. Men were asking us to roll dice, and celebrities like Keenan and Marlon Wayans were clearing paths as we strolled through the casino.

Near the blackjack tables, I saw NBA rookies Chris Webber and Jalen Rose, formerly of the University of Michigan's Fabulous Five. They were guards for the Denver Nuggets at the time.

I felt like a little girl in a candy store, picking out what I wanted for my sweet tooth. Chocolate men were everywhere. I was also amazed to find out that alcohol was free in the casino as long as you were over twenty-one and gambling.

Finally, after walking almost the entire casino, I was approached by a guy who happened to be with Mike Tyson's camp. He handed me three red laminated passes to Mike Tyson's cookout that Sunday, along with three T-Shirts for the event.

"Cool. Thanks buddy!" I said, grinning.

The T-Shirts had "Mike Tyson's First Annual Cookout Sunday, 8/20/1995" on the front. The back listed names of NBA players and celebrities that were scheduled to attend.

"Where'd you get those passes from?" I heard Asia's girls say, running up behind me as soon as the man disappeared. "Get us some!"

All I knew was that I'd come with two other females, so that was all I got.

That night we tried to attend a couple of parties, including one promoted by Asia's NBA friend, Alonzo Mourning. While we waited with her to enter his party, Alonzo showed up hand-in-hand with another female. He made Asia look like an idiot by totally ignoring her in front of all of us. Her face was so red that I felt bad for her. That night, I promised myself no dude would ever play me like that. I had never been more wrong in my life.

CHAPTER 3

The girls and I had no choice but to call it a night and go back to our hotel room when we couldn't get into Asia's friend's party. I changed into my pajamas and came out of the bathroom to find that the girls had taken up all the space in the two queen-size beds. I didn't even feel like getting into it with them bitches, so I got a pillow and blanket and slept on the floor, all the while feeling like I had been punked.

The next day I barely said a word to any of the girls. I really wanted to hang out by myself, but I tried to remain cool enough to make sure I got a ride back to Los Angeles when it was time to go.

But Diamond had other plans. She took me aside and asked if I wanted to hang with her by myself. I was like, "Cool." Later that evening after the Tyson fight, Diamond and I met up with a friend of hers at the MGM. He was a former NBA player named Walt.

Walt was a graduate of St. John's University, and prior to playing overseas, he had a short stint as a forward in the NBA with teams like the San Antonio Spurs, the New Jersey Nets, and the Houston Rockets. He was with his cousin, whose name I can't remember.

Me, Diamond, Walt, and his cousin all jumped into a limosine and wound up at some strip club that had nothing but Caucasian and Asian chicks stripping. The music sucked, but I wasn't ready to call it a night, considering I would probably be sleeping on the floor anyway.

By the end of the night, Diamond and Walt had hit it off pretty good and decided we should head back to Walt's room.

Diamond and I ended up sleeping in Walt's room with him and his cousin. It was already clear that Walt and Diamond were going to get their thang on because they couldn't keep their hands off each other at the bar. I wanted to disappear because I was stuck with what's his name in the bed.

I tried to play dead next to Walt's cousin, who was short, broke, and ugly, but it didn't work. Finally I gave in because Walt and Diamond were moaning and groaning loudly and passionately enough that I actually got turned on. I figured I could let Walt's cousin have enough foreplay with me to get me off so I could fall asleep, and it worked.

The next day was Mike Tyson's cookout. I was rocking my new red T-shirt, which I had tied in a knot on one side. Sheila, Asia, and I drove the ten-mile stretch to Mike's Tuscan-style home. When we got to the door, we were ushered in and directed to the backyard through a set of sliding glass doors. There was catered food on tables to the right and several circular tables with white tablecloths and centerpieces surrounding the built-in pool that sat in the center of the backyard. There was even a DJ spinning records.

The weather was really gloomy and the temperature was only in the high sixties, so swimming was out of the question. I was just happy to be at Mike's home. After half an hour, Mike walked out and personally welcomed us. He was soft spoken, warm, and very hospitable. We congratulated him on winning his fight and thanked him for having us out.

After the first hour, one by one, celebrities started walking in. I saw Naughty by Nature and a few other New York cats who could've been Junior M.A.F.I.A. Walt eventually showed up, and, surprisingly, he knew most of the NYC crew.

The party was cool, but after being there a couple of hours, I was ready to leave besides, only a handful of celebrities came through and they were mostly New Yorkers. And I didn't mean just the party—I was ready to leave Las Vegas. The trip wasn't really what I had expected, and Walt had started flirting with me right in front of Diamond, so I knew it was time to get out of there.

The girls and I agreed to leave the party, but Sheila told me that she and Asia weren't ready to go back to LA. She suggested that I hang out at the MGM casino until she and Asia were ready to make the drive back. It sounded fishy but reluctantly agreed to meet back up with them in the lobby of the MGM hotel two hours from the time they dropped me off.

While I waited I decided to walk over to Caesar's Palace to meet up with a guy from Atlanta that I'd met the previous day. While we were talking, we heard that a fight had broken out at the MGM Grand: there were gunshots, and some folks had even been robbed. By the time I got back there, the lobby was empty, and the girls I was supposed to ride back to LA with were nowhere in sight.

I wandered around the casino, looking for them for an hour, finally realizing those bitches had left, and I was stranded. I had no luggage, not much money, and no ride back home.

I was scared, worried, and didn't know what the fuck to do. I stumbled around for another half hour, trying not to cry, when out of nowhere a guy approached me. He pointed to his name on the back of my T-Shirt. It was Jalen Rose, the point guard for the Denver Nuggets.

Jalen told me he had been shooting craps and noticed me pacing back and forth for at least an hour. Still trying not to cry, I explained my situation to him. He chuckled a little, then asked me if I was hungry and if I could start at the top of my story over a meal.

Jalen and I hit up one of the buffets and feasted as I explained how my girls had just vanished without me. He felt bad and told me not to worry because he had just hit it big on the crap table and would help me out.

Jalen not only took me to the airport to purchase my ticket back to Los Angeles, but he even put $500 in my pocket. I must say that for my very first pro athlete encounter, he surely was a blessing.

When I got back to Los Angeles to get my belongings from Sheila, I made sure that I had one of my goons with me just in case she tried to get fly at the mouth. When I asked her what happened, she had the nerve to talk shit as if I had done something wrong to her SpongeBob ass. She didn't even have an explanation or an apology. I truly believe she let those females we shared the room with take my seat the way they'd taken my bed.

But I would get over it easily because it was this trip that really set the stage for the events that soon followed. The men I had encountered would eventually send for me around the globe, exposing me to worlds I had never seen, so I couldn't possibly stay mad at SpongeBob for long.

Was It Because I Swallowed

CHAPTER 4

It wasn't until I'd arrived back in Virginia from Las Vegas that I learned how easy it was to get next to celebrities.

My friend Michelle, whom I'd met at a nightclub when I returned to Richmond for my second year of college, was a very nice, semicute dark-skinned chick from Freeport, New York. Michelle had an extralong weave, a huge ass, and a tiny waistline. She invited me to Virginia State University to see a tour that her homeboy, Arnold, aka LS1, happened to be DJing for.

Michelle and I were geeked because the tour, called The Show, featured rappers Onyx, Method Man, Redman, and the whole Wu Tang Clan. Near the end of the performances, Michelle and I were on stage during the very popular "Ice Cream" song performance. Michelle was dancing on top of one of the speakers, and I was on the other speaker across the stage, shaking what my grandma gave me.

The next day, Michelle and I hooked up again with LS1 and his friend Mathematics, aka Math, this time in Richmond at their hotel twenty minutes from the Virginia State venue. Most of the artists from the tour had rooms on the same floor as LS1's.

Math, who was Method Man's brother, handed me his room key and asked if I'd go out and get some goodies. Immediately I left to pick up some chronic bud and alcoholic beverages. When I came back an hour later, the hotel hallway was filled with people going in and out of rooms. Some of the room doors were wide open, as if it was one big party, so I walked from room to room, looking for Michelle, LS1, and Math and yelling out their names.

The next thing I knew, Puffy Combs appeared out of nowhere with a cocky attitude. At the time, I didn't know who he was because he was up-and-coming in the music industry. He asked his security guard, "Who is she, and what is she doing?" As if I was singled out by him or something.

I kept walking; then I heard him say, "Motherfucking groupies always looking for Meth."

"Just because I was dancing on speakers yesterday?" I thought to myself. He told his security guard to ask me to leave the floor. I turned around and said, "I don't know who you are, but I have a key card to be in this hotel just like you, so you best get the fuck out my face! And by the way, I'm looking for Math—as in Mathematics—not Meth as in Method Man." Then I stormed off.

When I finally found Michelle, LS1, and Math, they had joined Sticky Fingaz and Fredro from Onyx in a room where some folks were smoking blunts and drinking. I walked in to chill with them, and immediately Sticky Fingaz began flirting. I liked it. I didn't even know him, and already I was considering getting with him—and at that time he was only a well-known rapper, not the rapper turned actor that ultimately made it to the big screen. Within the hour he must've realized I had given him the green light because he grabbed my hand and walked me to his hotel room, quickly closing the door behind him. Once we made our way over to the king-size bed, we got *it* in, just like groupies do. Afterward, I swallowed the blame because Sticky and I had just met. It wasn't his fault he didn't even have to work at getting my goodies. But at that moment nothing mattered because he was a famous rapper. "This is what they do while on tour," I told myself.

I didn't care if we ever saw each other again because I was just living for that moment.

The next concert I attended was with my cousin Minga. We had front-row seats to see the O'Jays at the Richmond Civic Center.

I had grown to realize that wherever I went, I had a body and face that could get any man's attention, broke, rich, young, or old. If I caught a man looking my way and I thought he was sexy and wanted some ass, or especially if he was paid, he would end up with me.

Earlier at the concert, having caught the eye of the lead singer, Eddie Levert Sr., we were escorted backstage by security to meet him after the performance. Although Eddie was old enough to be my granddaddy, I wasn't going to pass up the opportunity to hang out with any celebrity. I had now started perfecting my celebrity-nabbing game, and I knew hanging out with any one of the Leverts would come with perks, even if it was just partying for the night for free. I would take what I could get and see what happened, even if it meant having to swallow the misogynistic bullshit that usually came later.

After the introduction we went to his luxurious penthouse suite and dined on good food, top-shelf alcohol, and marijuana that came straight from Hawaii.

We were eventually joined by my friend Michelle and Eddie's son, Gerald. Gerald immediately began making jokes about Michelle's and my big butts. Later, Eddie tried to push up on me and was shocked that I wasn't interested in his old ass. I wasn't exactly sure what I was getting myself into, but I had a feeling that I would have to swallow the arrogance of some artists, like Gerald Sr., who think they can have any groupie they want just because they are celebrities.

After that night, I decided it was time for me to broaden my horizons and get down with real celebrities. During my sophomore year, I'd befriended a girl named Liz I'd met at a party. Liz was tall, thin, light skinned, and cute. She quickly became my new partner in crime.

One night we drove to Washington, DC, to hang out. When we got to the club, it was already popping. I never saw so many professional and military black men congregating like that in my life. The DC nightlife had it going on.

Certain parts of the club were darker than other sections, so I wasn't sure if I was seeing correctly. But I saw someone from a distance, and he looked pretty damn good. The closer I got, the nicer he looked. He was tall, dark, athletic, and handsome—just the way I liked them.

I could also see that people were gesturing toward him as if he was someone important. He looked bothered by all the attention. This stallion of a man was standing next to his homeboy, who was engaged in a conversation with a woman. By the way all the heads were turning when me and my girl walked in the club, I knew I was the finest chick in there, so I decided to step to the handsome brotha and introduce myself.

His name was Jackson, and he was six foot three inches and 220 pounds of pure chocolate. Jackson said he was a rookie wide receiver with the Washington Redskins.

I did all the talking. He didn't say much, but apparently he liked what he saw. By the end of the night, I was going wherever Jackson went. I made sure I didn't lose sight of him. Liz and I knew we didn't want to drive the one hundred or so miles back to Richmond that night. Not to mention, neither one of us wanted to get a driving-while-intoxicated charge. Trying not to sound too needy, I asked Jackson if Liz and I could spend the night with him.

What man says no to not one but two females? Even though we all slept in our clothes in the same queen-size hotel room bed, I made sure Liz's long arms or legs didn't accidentally cross mine and grab any part of Jackson. That was my candy, and I wasn't intending to share.

Nothing happened between me and Jackson that night, but we did manage to sneak in a kiss here and there while Liz slept. The next morning we exchanged phone numbers, and he invited me to come back and visit him at his home in the near future.

The following week, Jackson phoned and sounded very eager to see me. He'd finally purchased a home and invited me to visit him sooner than later.

The weekend after that phone conversation, I drove back to DC to see him. The neighborhood he lived in wasn't too far from the Tyson's Corner shopping district, a well-known wealthy area in DC.

When I arrived, Jackson was outside at the top of his steps at the front door as if he'd been anxiously awaiting my arrival. He gave me a long, tight hug, and then we walked inside.

He gave me a tour of his home, and I remember thinking there was really nothing spectacular about the place—until we got to the basement. I got excited just like a little kid because there was a large game room with a life-size electronic race car game, pinball, and Pac-Man game machines inside. It was the first time I had seen an in-home arcade.

We headed up the two flights of stairs to his master suite. It was unlike anything I'd ever seen. Inside the bedroom I could see the bathroom through the french doors. The huge bathtub was in the middle of the bathroom, which seemed an awkward place for it. There were lit candles everywhere—on the counter tops and even the edges of the bathtub. All that was missing were rose petals.

I decided to steal a kiss. He was just so fine that I couldn't keep my tongue off him, so we got busy. We continued to kiss, taking off all of our clothes at the same time. It was like we couldn't wait for each other. He inserted his chocolate dipstick inside me and started to ram me. Although I enjoyed it, it wasn't enough. I wanted more and more. I was worried he couldn't keep up because I wanted to be sexed up all night, but he didn't.

The next day when it was time for me to go, I asked him for cash to drive back to Richmond. His mood seemed to shift. I was a student, and unlike some of the girls I went to college with, I didn't come from a rich family or have a daddy that was paid. As far as I was concerned, he was a well-paid rookie in the NFL that I'd given my goods to, so the least he could do was cough up some of that cash, even if it was only a few hundred. So what I swallowed my pride when he handed me three one hundred dollar bills. I needed the money, and I assumed he had more than enough to go around.

Over the next few months, I continued to see him every so often, but I knew our relationship wasn't going anywhere.

Meanwhile, back in Richmond I knew my days were numbered in that boring city. Sure, I was in school, but that didn't mean I didn't need excitement.

Out of nowhere, Barry, one of the guys I'd met in Las Vegas, called and invited me to Atlanta for New

Year's. I wanted to go because I'd never been to Georgia. Besides, who wants to ring in the New Year in Richmond when she can be in Atlanta?

Barry was well over six feet, brown skinned, and less attractive than I would have liked, but very kind nonetheless. He lived in Memphis. I wasn't sure what he did for a living at the time, and frankly I didn't care because he'd already purchased my plane ticket.

Shortly after checking into our hotel room, Barry took me to the Lenox Mall in Buckhead to find me a New Year's Eve outfit. I remember skipping around like a ten-year-old when he told me to pick whatever I wanted because price didn't matter.

Later that evening we attended the New Year's Eve party at the Fernbank Museum. There was plenty to drink, the music was great, and the people were interesting. Barry and I were having a wonderful time up until we counted down to ring in 1996. Thirty minutes later, the crowd swelled from maybe a hundred people to easily five times that many. When the bar ran out of alcohol, we both knew it was time to go. People were becoming rude, and the concrete floor was so slick from so many spilled drinks that I almost busted my ass.

We then went to a club called Club 112 on Cheshire Bridge. I almost lost my mind, it was so crunk. Local talents were posted up, like Ludacris and his then sidekick, Poon Daddy. Ludacris went by the name Cris Lover Lover then. The music stayed popping, the drinks never dried up, and the weed stayed in the air. We didn't leave until six in the morning. It was so much fun that I promised myself I would go back one day.

I really enjoyed bringing in the new year with Barry because he was such a gentleman; not once did he try to touch me. My trip to Atlanta made such an impact on me that when I finished my sophomore year, I decided to relocate there.

Just before I packed up to move to Atlanta, Walt—the guy Diamond was making out with that night in Vegas while I was with his ugly cousin—invited me to visit him in Greece. He purchased a first-class round-trip ticket to Athens for me and even sent me $500 to apply for a passport. I was really anxious to get to Greece and find out more about Walt. No one had ever sent for me from such a far distance, and I wanted to know if there was more money where that came from.

He was eagerly waiting for me at the airport. Our interaction was awkward at first, but the more we talked, the more I warmed up to him. Within a couple of days, we were intimate. I tried not to remember all the moaning Diamond was doing when they'd had sex a year earlier in Vegas. However, I did wonder why she was moaning so loudly, because there wasn't much to moan about.

As my first international trip, Athens turned out to be a gold mine travel destination, especially with its vast historical sites. Too bad I forgot to pick up a guidebook; otherwise I wouldn't have shown up in a minidress and high-heeled shoes to visit the Parthenon. We had to walk up the steepest hill of nothing but rocks and rubble to see the temple, the oldest piece of temple history, created in 447 BC. This trip was my first experience of what life was like outside of America. So, of course, when the following year Walt offered me another trip—this one to Milan, Italy—I took it. That is every model's, designer's, and fashionista's dream! Besides, traveling first-class got me hooked! I loved spending time on his condominium balcony every day, drifting off to the sounds and the smell of the Mediterranean Sea. By the end of my week-long visit, I didn't want to go, but I needed to start packing to relocate to Atlanta. I knew that I definitely couldn't live another year in Richmond.

Was It Because I Swallowed

CHAPTER 5

My brother James lived in Atlanta, so when I got there, the first thing I did was visit him. I hadn't seen Little James since he was nine years old, and there was nothing little about him anymore. He was over six feet tall and weighed over 200 pounds. James had just graduated from Clark Atlanta University and agreed to let me crash on his couch for a couple of weeks, until I was able to find a place to live.

I wasted no time, immediately applied to Georgia State University, and easily got accepted for the 1996 fall quarter. My next step was to find work, which wasn't difficult either, considering Atlanta was the host of the Summer Olympics that year and jobs were in abundance.

Within my second week, I was able to find a place to stay. I had met a guy who needed someone to occupy his house because he traveled often and was afraid his home would get broken into when he was away. At $250 per month, I was his girl.

It was a five-bedroom, three-bathroom, fully furnished ranch-style home with a built-in pool and a game room. It was perfect!

It didn't take long for me to realize that I was in the right place: Atlanta was raining celebrities. I was meeting and rolling with celebrity after celebrity after celebrity. While Atlanta welcomed the world for the Olympics, I was trying to win a gold medal by coming up on as many celebrities as possible.

I met Shaquille O'Neal while waitressing at Dugan's Sports Bar. We later met up at another spot, called Frozen Paradise, on Memorial Drive in Stone Mountain.

During our conversation Shaq asked about my background and my goals and seemed quite interested in what I was saying. When he asked if I'd ever been married, I knew I was making strides with what I hoped would be my own personal million-dollar bill.

All of a sudden, we were rudely interrupted: two black chicks wearing hair extensions and chewing gum excessively had the nerve to sit down at our table as if I didn't exist.

I wasn't trying to get an assault charge that night for beating the bitches off, so I told Shaq I had to leave and we would talk later when the vultures weren't around. I went back home, all the while wishing I had stayed. I told myself I would never again give up that easily on what could've been my golden ticket.

I quickly got over Shaq when Charlie, who played third base for the Pittsburgh Pirates, called a week later to tell me he would be in Atlanta and would love to see me. I'd met Charlie during an adventure to Philadelphia with Liz a year earlier. Charlie flew me to Pittsburgh for a couple of days of mediocre sex, but he was still cool.

When Charlie arrived in Atlanta, he took me to lunch, where we had the usual idle chat. We then drove to Circuit City, where he purchased a Zenith thirty-two-inch color television for me. Charlie said he would love to see me at the game to watch him play against the Atlanta Braves and handed me a ticket.

At the game, I had a great seat really close to the field. While watching the game, I spotted the Braves's rookie outfielder, Jay, who was practicing in the batting area a short distance from me. While he was hitting almost every baseball that came his way, I walked back and forth, pretending to be lost, hoping to get his attention. I knew I was looking fly in my knitted cream-colored short-sleeved belly shirt that I'd purchased in Greece. I was betting that if I caught Jay's eye, he would like what he saw.

I was right. Five minutes later, a stadium employee came up to me and gave me Jay's number.

I called Jay later that evening, and we arranged to hook up the following day. I picked him up at Turner Field—the Braves's baseball park—and we went to hang out at Dave and Buster's, a restaurant, bar, and arcade in Marietta.

Jay was caramel, tall, and very well put together. I couldn't keep my eyes off him. After eating dinner and playing a few games, we both had sex on the brain and decided to bounce.

Being a rookie, Jay had been taken under the wing of a veteran Braves player who was living with his wife and two kids in Fayetteville, just south of Atlanta, near Evander Holyfield's mansion. We decided to go there, and as soon as we arrived, we went to Jay's room downstairs in the basement and fucked like rabbits. He'd been rubbing up against me at the restaurant while we were shooting baskets, so I sort of knew he was packing. When I finally got to the goods, it was thicker than I'd expected and big, just the way I like it. "I would never get tired of this fine ass," I thought to myself.

We continued to see each other regularly, and every time we fucked like there was no tomorrow. As a matter of fact, one of the reasons the Braves made it to the World Series that year was that Jay was so light on his feet as an outfielder—and not without a little help from me.

But I was getting a bad vibe. Whenever I came over, Jay always seemed to sneak me into his room in the basement through the garage. I never walked through the front door and never stepped one foot upstairs. I felt like a slave or the help who could only enter through the rear. I felt that he only saw me as a hoochie. Of all the nights we slept together—and there were a few of them—he only asked me to sleep over once.

I began to think that maybe he already had a girlfriend. But because he was so fine and the sex was so off the meter, I put off asking him about it.

Reluctantly I had to swallow the fact that every visit with Jay, he would sneak me into the house through the garage. Later he was traded to the Kansas City Royals. I never heard from him after that, only further substantiating that I was nothing but a piece of ass to him.

I was getting to have sex with some major players, but I wasn't getting anything of value in return. I needed to come up, make some money for my skills. I told myself that if I was going to be treated the way Jay treated me, I was going to have to start being about the money.

I used to see the rapper Too Short at all the hot spots my first year in Atlanta, but I wasn't introduced to him until R. Kelly's 1997 New Year's Eve party at the old House of Blues.

Even though R. Kelly failed to perform that night, I bumped into Too Short, and Short and I decided to exchange numbers.

We started to hang out, sometimes just to smoke blunts, but more often as friends; he even taught me to shoot pool. One evening while out on the town, I ran into him at Club 112. It was five in the morning, and out of the blue he just up and asked me if he could have sex with me.

"Sure, for some dough, of course," I said as casually as he'd asked me. We left together, and I followed him to an ATM by his house, where he withdrew $500. I didn't care about having sex for money because I was a student and every penny mattered. At least that's what I told myself. Besides, I loved sex, so if I got money for doing something I enjoyed, it was a bonus.

To my surprise, Too Short was packing in the meat department, if you know what I mean. He and I had sex multiple times that morning, from the Jacuzzi to his bed, and each time I got my rocks off.

Weeks later when I saw Too Short out, he said, "Where's my $500? I want a refund." After I didn't respond, he said, "Well, what about a discount for another round?" I had to take a deep breath and swallow the shame of being paid for sex by someone who rapped about pimping. It felt quite awkward, actually, but I played it off because I did consider Short a homeboy of mine—with benefits.

Months later, I met NBA player Dee, one of the first African ball players to ever play for the Atlanta Hawks, outside the old Atlanta Live nightclub parking lot. He approached me in his Mercedes. Dee was seven two, over 240 pounds, and had played center for the Atlanta Hawks. He had a very thick African accent, and I admit he wasn't easy on the eyes by any means, but he definitely was paid, which was all that mattered. He could've had one eyeball; as long as he kept it on me, it was all good.

Dee and I eventually hooked up later that week for lunch. Over lunch he told me about how much he loved children and how much he donated to them through his charities. With that in mind, I wanted to hook up with him, my sole intention being to solicit his help for my four little cousins living in Rhode Island with a struggling, drug-addicted mother. It was just weeks before Christmas 1997, and I knew if he didn't help, my little cousins would have a horrible holiday.

I asked Dee to put on his Save the Children cape and take me to Toys"R"Us. And just like that, he did. We spent well over $1,000 on dolls, toys, and games for my little cousins.

To this day I will never forget Dee's looking out for my family like that. But that wasn't the only thing I won't forget. When we did hook up again, we had sex, and his stuff was so big it could've been used as a weapon. Afterward I had to swallow the damage because he assaulted my vagina in the process.

After Dee I ended up running into another NBA center, Big E, who had just been traded by the Los Angeles Lakers to the Charlotte Hornets. We met at Club 112, where he was with another NBA center, Eric Dampier. Big E immediately caught my eye because he was big—six foot eleven and around 250 pounds—and attractive. Big E and I hit it off. We had great chemistry and started sexing it up in only a matter of days. Initially he told me that if I ever needed anything to just ask. A few months later, I made my annual trip to LA and let Big E know that I was in town. He immediately invited me out to his Redondo Beach two-story Spanish-style home with ocean views. It was prime real estate.

As Big E gave me a tour of his home, I mentioned that I would be in need of some cash to pay for my trip and asked him if he could help me out. He told me it wouldn't be a problem. With that in mind, I broke it down and began undressing so we could get busy.

After steamy sex, as I put my clothes back on, he asked me, "Are you going to be doing some shopping?" It sounded as if he were offering.

I said, "Yes, I would love to." There was a huge pause on his end. I figured he would go into his wallet and pull out some benjamins for me. The money would be much appreciated. But Big E didn't go into his wallet.

Had he forgotten that he once told me that if I ever needed something to just ask? As my nostrils began to flare, I envisioned myself busting up everything in his bedroom. I thought about grabbing a sculpture and smashing his big-screen television or throwing his remote controls and smashing the picture frames on his bedroom walls. I was pissed! I had to snap out of it and swallow the fact that I couldn't do any of that.

As he walked me downstairs toward the front door, he handed me $200, exactly what I needed to pay for my weekly car rental. I made sure that there was never a next time with his buster ass.

Not much longer after that Los Angeles trip I ran into Sean, an Atlanta native who played guard/forward for the Utah Jazz. He stood six foot six and tilted the scales at over 200 pounds. He met my minimal requirements of being cute, large, and energetic. He was fun to talk to, really understood me, and seemed genuinely interested in me.

When Sean and I began to kick it, I don't think he had any idea of what he was getting himself into. Once when we were at Club Otto's in Buckhead ordering drinks at the bar, I began to fondle him. We hadn't even had sex yet, but the club was so crowded that I didn't think anyone could see what I was doing. I unzipped his pants and tried to stroke his dick. It was so funny to me. I wish I could have captured the stunned, deer-in-the-headlights look on his face. After we drank up, he said he was ready to go.

It was on and popping with us immediately. Sean tasted like butterscotch candy. I needed to find out if I had anything other than sex in common with him because he was a keeper.

I think he might have been thinking the same about me because he invited me to hang out in Salt Lake City where he played for the Utah Jazz. He picked me up from the airport and drove me to his apartment to unload my luggage before we drove to the Delta Arena, where his team played. I was in awe of the scenery: I had absolutely no idea that Utah was so beautiful.

The mountaintops were covered with snow and visible from almost anywhere I stood in the city. I saw Amish people driving carriage-led horses. I thought I was in an old Western movie or something.

When we got to the arena, I found out that it was Fan Appreciation Day, so the local kids and their parents were playing games and interacting with his Utah Jazz teammates, including Karl Malone and Brian Russell.

After an hour or so, Sean and I bounced because we had unfinished business back at his apartment. When we got back, we had sex immediately. I couldn't wait another minute. It was just like the first time. Awesome!

We later hung out at a local restaurant with some of his teammates for food and drinks.

I really enjoyed my couple of days in Salt Lake City with him, but when the season was over, Sean returned to Atlanta and suddenly stopped calling me. I swallowed that sadness, and eventually I got over it.

It all worked itself out for me because I seemed to be in demand by NBA players for some reason. Not too long after I dated Sean, I ran into the Denver Nugget's power forward, Ant.

Tall, dark, and extremely handsome, he was definitely a pleasant surprise. I happened to be driving in the Buckhead area of Atlanta and decided to ride by Club Otto's. Ant was standing in front of the club, in the same spot where all the drama had popped off with NFL player Ray Lewis, who was charged and later acquitted in the stabbing death of a man.

Ant had on a white button-down shirt with a sweater vest on top, starched jeans, and very expensive shoes. He looked like money. I pulled up beside him in my 1998 Toyota 4Runner to see him grinning from ear to ear. I asked him how he liked the club. Lucky for me, he didn't. I asked him, "Would you like to join me instead?"

He jumped in my SUV, and we took off. I took him to my loft at the Fulton Cotton Mill on Boulevard to see the view from the rooftop, which was one of the most amazing city views in Atlanta at that time. We ended up conversing on the rooftop almost until the sun came up, and then I took him back to his hotel.

Ant returned a few weeks later and invited me to visit him at the Ritz Carlton in downtown Atlanta. When I entered his room, I immediately developed an itch that only he could scratch. He was sexy, and his calm demeanor made him easy prey. I began to kiss him, first on the lips, and then I worked my way downward toward his neck. I didn't stop there. I began kissing on his shoulders, slowly removing his clothes. By this time, he was looking so well equipped below the waist that I almost lost my balance trying to rip his clothes off to get to it. Ant's touch was gentle and unforgettable. I had an orgasm almost immediately after he entered me. Afterward, he and I didn't even get the chance to cuddle because Nick Van

Exel, his teammate, was knocking on his hotel door, forcing Ant to cut our time together.

Ant and I were supposed to meet up later that evening but didn't. A few weeks later, Ant was back in town when he called me. Immediately we met up again and had sex. After a few times of meeting up just for sex, I realized that every time he came to town, he would call me just for that reason and nothing else. The last time we met up was at the Marriott Marquis in downtown Atlanta. And once again we went straight to having sex. We were supposed to meet up later to go out, but that never happened.

Soon I had to swallow the thought that this could possibly be his MO. I tried to convince myself that it was all good because he'd at least hit me off with a few hundred dollars every time we met. But it wasn't good because my feelings were hurt.

Eventually I lost interest and moved on. One night months later, I ran into him. He looked good. He also looked happy to see me. We started talking as if nothing had gone wrong between us. I could sense that he still had fire in his groin for me, but it was too late. I'd used an extinguisher to put out his flame in my heart a long time ago.

Was It Because I Swallowed

CHAPTER 6

It wasn't just NBA players that were all over Atlanta, but NFL players as well. For a minute it seemed as though I was coming up more on the football players than my NBA come-ups.

I was beginning to have sex with pro football player after pro football player. I couldn't get enough. It was like an addiction.

Every time a player wanted to have sex with me, it was a high, like drugs hitting the bloodstream. I should've felt bad, giving up my body like that every time a pro player looked my way. Instead, I kept looking for a new fix.

With swarms of women in the clubs, I loved the fact that these rich, balling-out players focused their attention on me. The voice in my head kept screaming that I needed to stop, but I shut that voice out, ignored what made sense, and continued to care only about what felt good. To this day, I think I should have had an intervention.

My physical attraction to pro-league players, or any celebrity for that matter, seemed to lead nowhere except to casual sex with them in whatever city they were in at the time.

After a while I started to feel empty inside. Even though most of them were generous with their money and showed me a good time at parties and restaurants, I really had no idea what I wanted from them other than a handout and some good sex.

I thought I might have benefited from a relationship, but I didn't know how to lock any of these guys down and be their girlfriend. I got so blinded by the glitter and gold that came with being in their presence that I feared being rejected and kicked to the curb if I mentioned wanting more than sex and a few hundred bucks. But after being broken off with cash after sex so often, I eventually told myself that I was worth more than that. I decided I should start demanding more from these men than just dick and dollars.

Dark skinned, six foot one, over 190 pounds, and attractive, Dale was a cornerback for the Kansas City Chiefs. I met him at the bar of Justin's Restaurant. Justin's was an upscale urban restaurant owned by Sean "Puffy" Combs. It had opened in Atlanta a few months earlier. At the time, Justin's was the new "it" spot, and every time I went there, the house was packed. My friend Lydia and I were lucky to even get a seat at the bar that particular night. While we were discussing how we'd be celebrating my thirty-first birthday, Dale must have overheard us. Why else would he have ordered me a shot of the most expensive brandy, Louis XIII? "My alcohol hero," I thought.

I gracefully accepted the gift, but it wasn't until after I'd toasted and taken the shot straight to the head that I realized it was $150 a pop. I overheard the bartender asking Dale if he was sure about bringing me another because they were so pricey.

"I sure am. It's her birthday!" he said.

I had no choice but to interrupt Dale, telling him he really didn't have to. "If you feel that obligated, then you could just give me the one-fifty instead?" I laughed, playing it off, but I wasn't joking.

He told me not to worry about it and sent it to me anyway, as if he had an endless flow of cash. I later found out he had just signed with the Denver Broncos.

After drinking two shots worth the same as my car payment that was already late, I was starting to feel a bit tipsy. Dale had a limo waiting outside and was on his way to the Gentlemen's Strip Club. He asked if we'd join him.

"Hell yeah!" I shouted.

Lydia and I packed up our belongings, jumped into his limo, and headed toward the club, like kids on our way to an amusement park.

At that time the Gentlemen's Club was the hottest black strip club in Atlanta. The white girls at the infamous Gold Club didn't have anything on these badass sistas.

On the main floor dozens of naked and nearly naked women of all shades were giving dances to the male and female patrons. The dancers had on six-inch heels, hair extensions, jewelry, and thongs. There were two stripper poles on the three-foot-high stage in the center of the room, where the female dancers tried to outdance one another. Upstairs was a more intimate setting, with couches and tables for private dances.

It was my birthday, and I was crunk. The night just kept getting better, especially after Dale handed me $1,000 in single dollar bills to splurge on the dancers. Although over the years I graduated to carrying gym bags full of money in the strip clubs for people like Pac Man Jones, I thought $1,000 was an awful lot at that time.

Of course I pocketed half of it, gave Lydia about a hundred, and then handpicked the strippers I wanted to see dance for Dale. I couldn't care less about females dancing for me because I had never been attracted to women even though lesbianism was starting to become quite popular in Atlanta. Eventually I learned to shake my own ankles to make my booty clap just in case I was asked to dance privately for someone. But I never could have stripped for a living because I feared my mom, aunties, or uncles up north would hear about it, pile in a van, head down south, and whoop my ass in the middle of a routine.

The evening with Dale turned out awesome. The music was hot, and the drinks never stopped coming. After a couple of hours of exotic entertainment, I knew it was time for us to go. Besides, I was drunk and not feeling well. I gave Dale my number, and I thanked him for making my birthday so memorable. He gave me more money for Lydia and me to take a cab back to my car that was still parked at Justin's.

The next day, as I joyfully drove around town, paying bills with my birthday money from Dale, he called and asked if I'd be available for dinner soon one evening.

"Sure, when?" I said.

"How about tonight?" he asked.

Even though it was almost six in the evening when we spoke, I agreed. I rushed home, showered, and searched my walk-in closet for the sexiest dress and shoes I had. I wore a sleeveless colorful silklike chiffon dress that was gathered around the top and middle but loosely fitted below the hip and stopped just before my kneecaps. I looked like a million dollars but didn't even have a steady bank account.

As I walked toward the exclusive steak house in downtown Atlanta to meet Dale, I started to wonder. I knew he had to have lots of money on him by the way he was flashing it the night before, but I didn't have a strategy to get any of it in my hands. Dale had it going on for himself, but I had no clue as to how to convince this man that I could be that one female he wanted to keep.

When I entered the restaurant, Dale was already seated in a private section. We embraced, sat down, and began talking about how much fun we'd had the night before. We ate and had such a good time at dinner that we decided to continue the conversation in his nearby hotel room.

Once in his room, we both knew what time it was. We were totally attracted to one another. The chemistry was definitely there.

Dale kissed on me as I kissed on him. We damn near tackled each other in the process. His soldier boy popped out of nowhere, practically tapping me on my shoulder because it was ready to play.

The sex was just as I thought it would be—great! But the best part was that he peeled me off a few hundred more dollars, even though I didn't ask for it. I guess I should have felt like a whore when I took the cash, but I didn't.

Though I needed the cash, I wanted him to ask me to spend the night with him more. Dale was a great catch for any woman, especially having just signed a multimillion-dollar NFL contract. I wished he'd ask me for my spare time. I wished he cared to probe into my dreams and aspirations, and I wished he wanted to grow with me as couples do, but none of that went down.

A few days later, I got a call from my close friend Shannon, telling me that Dale and I were seen together at the strip club. Since Shannon grew up in the same rural area in Georgia as Dale, word got back to her quickly.

My girl Shannon was real light skinned, attractive but country in a cute way. She informed me that her friend was already involved with Dale and very much pregnant, carrying his baby.

My heart was broken. I really thought I could've had something with Dale. I couldn't believe it. I didn't want to believe it, so I tried to rationalize a way that I could continue seeing him.

If he had been involved with some random chick, I could have swallowed that fact and kept on seeing him, putting the sex on him hard till he dropped the other girl. But since his baby's mother was a friend of a friend, I backed down.

Was It Because I Swallowed

CHAPTER 7

I continued running into pro athletes damn near on a daily basis. It was becoming senseless how many of them ended up being one-night stands, and if they weren't, they sure felt like it in the long run.

Kavika was a handsome Dallas Cowboy defensive end at six foot six and 270 pounds. He was charming, charismatic, and such a character that I thought he had the potential to one day become an actor. He was so full of life that when we met in the upstairs section of the Atlanta Live Club, I was immediately taken by his personality.

Kavika had been frequenting Atlanta because his brother lived there with his family. He was always joking and making fun of everything and everyone the way I always did, so we really hit it off. Whether we were talking about what someone was wearing in the grocery store or cracking on one another, we were always laughing.

Kavika loved to eat, drink, and have a good time. He would always treat me to the popular Atlanta restaurants, our favorite being just about any Mexican spot.

Kavika would want to have sex at the drop of a hat and almost anywhere. We could be on the highway driving, and if I started to talk sexy or fondle him while he was behind the wheel, he'd gun his big-body Mercedes, breaking all speeding laws, trying to find a spot to get busy. We were hooked on each other. I assumed he was single and available because whenever he was in town, we were inseparable.

After the first month or so, I decided we'd reached the point in our friendship where it was time to ask him about his life in Texas. Sadly for me, Kavika admitted that he had just had a baby boy back in Dallas. I automatically assumed that he had to have some kind of relationship with his baby's momma because his son was less than a year old. When I asked about the mother, he said there was nothing between them. I don't know why, but after hearing that, for some reason I just assumed he didn't even have a girlfriend.

However, after Kavika returned to Atlanta from an extended stay in Dallas, something about him wasn't the same, and he seemed distant. He had forgotten what I liked and disliked sexually. He acted as if he wasn't familiar with my body anymore, surprising me during one sexual encounter by biting on me. When I screamed at him, he seemed surprised. I never liked any unnecessary roughness like that shit. At one time I could've sworn he knew that because he was so huge that he'd easily toss me around sometimes hurting me in the process.

What once seemed comfortable and connected now was awkward. It was as if he had been tampered with, but I brushed it off, pretending I was that woman that every man wanted and that he would be a fool to try to deal with someone else.

We continued to see each other whenever he had a break in his football schedule, but I should have sensed something was wrong when he failed to send me to Dallas the next NFL season.

He was then traded to the Denver Broncos, putting even further distance between us. After he relocated to Denver, he invited me there and I assumed he really must've had a girlfriend, making me just his Atlanta sidepiece.

However, I declined that trip because I wasn't Boo-Boo the Fool. If I had taken him up on that offer, I would've had to swallow the fact that I was his sidepiece for a second time.

After having had enough of being Kavika's sidepiece when I ran into another NFL player named Joc. He was so gorgeous that I had to do a double take when I saw him. After my last two NFL-player mishaps, I wasn't trying to talk to any others, but something about Joc just seemed right, from his looks to his conversation. He was only twenty-four when we met, so I told myself, "Be patient, get to know him—he could be the one."

We met during my very first visit to Miami. I was there to attend the Music Soul Festival in May 2001. We were at Club Marlin on Collins Avenue in South Beach. I was hanging out with my girls when I saw him across the room, and I thought, "Damn, who is this god?" He was stunning! I walked up to him and asked if I could suck his kneecaps. I had to look around myself slowly because I couldn't believe those words had actually come out of my mouth. I followed up with, "Didn't I see you on a box of Wheaties or something?" He busted out laughing.

BAM! I had him.

He was a black stallion. Sheer perfection. And his Colgate smile, oh my God! If I could've thanked his mom and dad by kissing them each on the forehead, I would have.

After we exchanged numbers, he made the booty call an hour or so later. I still had no idea who he was. He could have had just two wooden nickels, and I would have rubbed those suckers together and made fifty cents so we could be together.

Joc pulled up to my hotel in a Mercedes, and I trailed him in my Toyota 4Runner to his oceanfront condo. The car and the condo were two indications that he had more than two wooden nickels. Joc eventually told me that he was a defensive end for the Tennessee Titans and that he lived in Nashville. He was nicknamed the Freak because he was large and crazy quick, characteristics unusual for his position.

After a short moonlit stroll along the shore, we sat on the sand. I don't remember what we discussed because all I saw in front of me was a piece of meat. USDA prime choice, grade A. His kneecaps were exposed, so I went for it—I sucked his kneecaps.

I'd never sucked anyone's kneecaps before, but for some reason, I had an overwhelming urge to suck his. I guess it was because his whole body looked so tasty that the kneecaps seemed like a great starting point. After my tasting session, he grabbed my hand and led me upstairs to his condo.

We hastily went into the master bath, undressed, and jumped into the shower. His six-pack abs were so defined that I looked up toward the sky and thanked God for this man's birth. We lathered each other down, getting all fresh for what was to come.

He was shy and reserved, and I was a beast. His body was like Six Flags, and I was about to ride. As he lay on his back, any time he tried to move, I would push him back down and have my way with him by tasting every body part that I could. He seemed to enjoy it very much. We fucked each other so hard that when we finished, we were both breathing as if we had just run a marathon.

Our first night together was unbelievable. It was so full of hot, wet sex that I was infatuated with him. I left the next morning and headed back to Atlanta. After that first encounter and over the years, he and I got together every couple of months, and always on my birthday. I was completely under his spell. I knew he wasn't ready to commit, but neither was I.

Was It Because I Swallowed

CHAPTER 8

I'm not exactly sure why I was banking on my pro-athlete and entertainment associates to help me financially instead of using my hard-earned bachelor's degree to survive. Maybe it was because over the last four years, I had grown accustomed to eating at the nicest restaurants and practically living in the VIP section at all the hottest clubs in Atlanta. But I had to remind myself that it was my celebrity associates that were rich, not me. My ass still needed to work and to stop taking handouts.

As a freshman in college, I'd often thought about applying to law school. I thought about it again after graduation; I just wasn't sure if I was ready to commit to the countless hours of studying. Besides, I was in hanging-out, partying, and kicking-it mode and really believed I needed a break from the books. I also knew I wasn't willing to put forth the work it took to become a lawyer. I wouldn't be able to afford it anyway.

The sad part was that I really wanted a degree in forensics, but in 1996 Georgia State had yet to incorporate a forensics program. My chosen political science major had to be switched to criminal justice in order for me to graduate on time. That was a downer because I had no interest in criminal justice. And after $50,000 of loans and a semester of interning with the Federal Bureau of Prisons, helping inmates transition into the real world, I had no real job prospects or any desire to work in that field.

Both working the internship and attending a class field trip to Jackson State Prison reminded me of the prisons I'd visited when my ex-husband was incarcerated. The thought of having to witness so many brothers behind bars for the rest of my life didn't excite me.

I was screwed! While searching for my first postgraduate job, I decided to apply for administrative jobs and paralegal positions only. I landed my first position—a software applications trainer with a data systems company. My starting salary was $35,000 a year, and I thought I'd come up. It was the most money I had ever earned on a job.

I was responsible for implementing and teaching imaging software to the employees of the companies that purchased it. It went great for the first six months, until my friend Nakia and her rich Nigerian friends invited me to London for an all-inclusive trip and European shopping spree.

I knew Nakia's Nigerian friends had money when she picked me up in a brand-new 1998 Mercedes ML320 SUV they'd loaned her during their visit to the United States. At that time Nakia was driving a bucket of a car, a 1980s Dodge Omni. Her new Nigerian acquaintance, whose name I can't remember, had an older brother who was a politician in Nigeria. Nakia promised hanging out with her friends all weekend would pay off, even if the politician brother looked like a troll.

I convinced myself that even if I wasn't attracted to the man, I could still keep him entertained. And I'm sure glad I did. Within two days he spent almost $10,000 on me—more than any other man ever had. I bought a new washer and dryer, cleaned up some bad credit, purchased a Roth IRA and two money market accounts, and paid off an outstanding balance on pictures from my art collection that were already in the shop being mounted and framed. Did I mention the shopping sprees at Bed Bath & Beyond, Lenox Mall, and Phipps Plaza? I really hoped that he wasn't expecting anything in return because it wasn't gonna happen. Never. Ever. Ever!

One thing I did admire about the guy was that even though he was visiting, it was all about me and I liked that. It was awesome! So when Nakia informed me that she was going to London with them, I dropped everything, including that imaging job, to join her. Yes, I quit a job on the spot to get with some dude and take his money.

Mere days after she told me about the trip, we boarded a nonstop flight to London with her Nigerian boo.

It was early evening when we landed at London's Gatwick Airport and took a taxi to the Chelsea area of London to the two-bedroom flat apartment where we'd be staying.

We had barely a chance to adjust to the eight-hour time difference and no time to rest before Nakia's friend was dragging us to a local nightclub. It was OK because I was geeked to be among the Brits. This club seemed to be no different from the nightclubs in the States, with the exception of the people and their British accents.

The music was jumping, the bottles were popping, and people were having a hell of a time. Just as we were getting our groove on, we were approached by a big man who told us we had to go. He didn't even have a British accent. Instead, he sounded just like a New Yorker.

"Shit! Not me!" I mumbled. He wasn't about to punk me for my post.

I asked him why we had to go if we were the only three people seated in the VIP section. Because of my demeanor, he claimed I got smart with him. Next thing I knew, I was being removed from VIP and forced to step backward off the stage and around the banister that separated the VIP section.

"Ain't this a bitch," I thought. What had just happened? I tried to talk this big black hulk into letting me back in, but he told me it was too late. Busta Rhymes was on his way. I said, "Great, because I just met and exchanged numbers with Busta two weeks ago in the parking lot at Club 112 in Atlanta."

That didn't seem to faze him.

I asked the man again why we had to move if we were the only ones in VIP. Apparently, Busta had beef in London before, and this latest visit, the club wanted to prevent any altercations if possible. I told him we weren't going anywhere, and if anything did go down, we would have Busta's back because we were Americans. "I mean, why can't we all just get along?" I joked.

I must have pissed him off because he wasn't buying anything I was saying anymore, and he told me to get the hell out.

I turned, started walking, and yelled back over my shoulder, "Kiss my ass!"

Nakia was laughing her ass off when I looked up at her, still on the VIP stage that I no longer had access to. "Some friend you are," I thought to myself.

I swallowed the embarrassment and took a cab back to the flat, alone. The only fun I had that night was that I got to see the Royal Palace and wave at the Queen's guards along the way.

The next day, Nakia and I hopped on the subway and then took a two-story city bus to get around London. We even considered staying on the train and taking it to Paris once we found out that it was only a few hours away.

For a couple of days, we got to go out and explore London without our Nigerian friends. We tried not to act like tourists, going from store to store, but the stores were banging, and we had no shortage of money because we kept being stopped by African men, from Kenyans to Ethiopians.

One Nigerian guy bought us each a pair of designer sunglasses within minutes of meeting us. I picked out a pair of Guccis, and Nakia a pair of Dolce & Gabbanas. Another African man invited us to the Grosvenor House, where royalty from all over the world and other celebrities, like Michael Jackson, stayed during their visits. This Nigerian introduced us to a real African prince who was staying in the presidential suite. The prince was so taken by Nakia's beauty that he opened a suitcase full of money—both dollars and euros—and told her to take what she wanted. Her ass only took $1,000, which didn't make sense to me, considering the American dollar was only worth seventy cents to the euro at the time. Overall, this trip was so worth it that I had absolutely no regrets about walking out on my job.

Was It Because I Swallowed

CHAPTER 9

I returned from London and landed a better gig with a printing company. I was hired to help incorporate imaging into the company's already-established printing business. But that only lasted a few months, until I was offered a job as an imaging project manager for a technology company. Unfortunately, that didn't last long either because that company went out of business within the year.

In 2000 I landed my fourth job, a contracted project coordinator with a facility resources company. Everything was good until my best friend from Los Angeles, Tonya, invited me to Steve Harvey's Annual Hoodie Awards in Las Vegas. She told me she had hotel accommodations at the new Aladdin all taken care of and that all I needed to do was show up. Considering I had already earned some paid leave time, I decided to use one of my days off the Friday before the Hoodie Awards weekend.

I told my supervisor that I would be in North Carolina for the weekend attending to my sick aunt who had breast cancer. I told myself that how I spent my day off was none of my employer's business. Unfortunately, I learned the hard way that everything I did on my computer at work was property of the company. All the exchanged e-mails, airline confirmations, and itineraries exposed my lies. When I returned to work that following Monday, I was fired.

But I didn't give up. I tried my luck in corporate America one last time as a paralegal, but I kept screwing up because of my lack of legal experience and knowledge of case law. I was fired from that job within the first couple of months.

Finally, I had swallowed enough of that firing shit! I was only working to make someone else rich, anyway. If I didn't do something soon, I would be in serious financial trouble. I needed work that didn't involve my having to conform to the traditional nine-to-five. I had to do something because my routine of asking my acquaintances for money to make ends meet was beginning to get old. It had been OK when I was a college student, but it had been over two years since I'd graduated, and it was time to get my shit in order.

Just when I was at the end of my rope, my brother James suggested I read Michael Kiyosaki's *Rich Dad Poor Dad*. I did, and it made so much sense to me. In a nutshell, the author said that there were two men in his life that he considered fathers, and each taught him a different way to gain financial success. One dad—like many in my mom's generation—believed that a person needed to go to school, work for someone else, and then retire with a gold watch and a retirement package. However, the economy had since changed, so my potential for retirement seemed bleak. Mr. Kiyosaki's other dad, who was really his best friend's dad, believed that if a person worked hard doing something enjoyable, something that came naturally, the odds of being successful were much higher.

The only problem was that at that time, besides having sex, partying, and being an avid reader, there was nothing I was really good at. Well, maybe braiding hair.

My oldest brother, Jeffrey, who passed away in 1987, had many talents, including drawing, fashion designing, dancing, doing gymnastics, braiding, and roller-skating. As a kid I used to try to shadow whatever he happened to be doing at the time, but I couldn't keep up.

Jeffrey attended the Fashion Institute of Technology in New York City, and by the time he was twenty-two, he had lived in Los Angeles, Miami, and New York. When I was seven years old, he taught me how to cornrow hair. To this day I wonder if he ever knew the impact his lessons would have on me.

In the beginning he would demonstrate the process to me on my sister's head. One of those times I got on the floor and began applying the same technique to the strings hanging from the bedskirts just to see if I could do it. It worked because I moved on to my many dolls' heads. Once I got the technique down, I had no shortage of volunteers I could practice on; family and friends were all willing to let me braid them. By the time I began braiding comfortably on my own, my brother had become popular with his skills. When he left Rhode Island, he left a void I wasn't sure I could fill. But I guess I did OK because I never had any complaints.

But that was fifteen years earlier, and I hadn't braided a single head in all that time.

In 2000 a large percentage of African Americans, from pro basketball players to football players to rappers, artists, and even boxers were starting to rock braids. I heeded Mr. Kiyosaki's dad's beliefs and resurrected my hobby.

When I first started to braid again, the only style I could do was the basic straight back with no designs. However, I wanted to take braids to another level, and I figured if I incorporated what my hair stylist did at the salon, such as washing, conditioning, and blow-drying, then I could provide this service to my clients for at least forty dollars per person. It was a start.

The club scene seemed like the only way at the time

for me to get braid business. I only wanted to solicit business from guys, especially those with plenty of money. Even if they didn't rock braids, they may have had kids that did.

I wasn't too sure about my new business venture and held off on printing business cards. I wasn't sure I could commit to doing hair full time because the market was so new to me, so I continued to hit the Atlanta club scene, looking for enough potential clients to get started.

Around this time I was frequenting Club Kaya on Peachtree Street in Atlanta. This was when Earwax Music, the tire shop and car wash, was next door.

One night Frank Ski, a V-103 radio personality, had just started hosting his annual birthday bash at Club Kaya. While he was emceeing, he introduced a young chick who then got onstage and began to play the piano. She was light skinned with long, beaded braids that hung in her face so much that I could barely see her. When she began playing the piano, the whole audience froze to see what her next move would be. Finally, she began belting out one of Mary J. Blige's songs. "Who is this goddess?" I thought. She was young, beautiful, and a musical genius.

When she finally finished her selection of songs, the audience went bananas. So, of course, when she walked off stage, I ran over to introduce myself as an Atlanta braider.

It was Alicia Keys.

Although she never became a customer, she was nice enough to let me approach her. So what if I handed her a piece of a ripped brown paper bag with my phone number on it? She still smiled and took it. To me that was confirmation enough to buy business cards and move forward with my braiding plan.

Was It Because I Swallowed

CHAPTER 10

I had reached a point of no return: it was either now or never. I had to step out on faith, and it was all or nothing. First, I would have to convince those around me that I had a hidden talent. One of my girlfriends, Sabrina, gave me a try and let me braid her hair straight back, even adding hair extensions to the braids. I only charged her forty dollars. She was very happy with the results, especially because she couldn't even see where I began adding the fake hair strands. My secret was that I began braiding the real hair first; then I'd add small hair strands to the middle pieces randomly. In return she referred me to rappers 8Ball and Pusha T.

I received a call from 8Ball of 8Ball and MJG, a rap duo from Memphis, who asked if I could come to his hotel to do his hair. Walking into the W Hotel, just north of Atlanta in the Perimeter area, I tried to make the situation seem routine, comparing it to walking inside an office building to report to work. But I couldn't. This new chosen profession was at the opposite end of the spectrum. As I approached the door and knocked, I was nervous: after all, 8Ball would be my first rapper client. "He has an audience, so don't fuck up his head," was all I kept saying to myself. I had to swallow my nerves because they were all over the place by the time I reached the door. That's when a petite brown-skinned girl came to the suite door and invited me in. 8Ball walked out of the bedroom and said, "Hey, what's up? How are you?"

"Good," I replied.

8Ball was a heavyset dark-skinned brother with a friendly smile, whose huge frame suggested that he loved to eat. 8Ball and MJG had collaborated with such labels as Bad Boy Entertainment and Grand Hustle Entertainment. They had also worked with such artists as Three 6 Mafia and UGK, whose music I love.

I began to explain my braiding process to him, telling him about washing his hair and every other step leading up to the braiding, which was the last step. I asked him if he didn't mind getting his hair washed in the hotel's bathroom sink.

After I washed his head in the sink, I brushed in some conditioner, which I rinsed out five minutes later. I then blow-dried it with a professional handheld dryer, all the while holding a brush to help straighten out the hair as it dried. The next step was to grease his scalp as I parted the hair to start braiding. This process was basically what I used throughout my braiding career.

I had finished prepping him, but I had no idea what type of design to do on 8Ball's head because I didn't know any. All I knew was that I was being referred for a service I had almost forgotten and had yet to perfect.

As 8Ball sat between my legs on the floor, I silently prayed for guidance from somewhere to come out of this momentary fog. It was time for my creative juices to flow so I exhaled and made a part down the middle of his scalp, then divided each side into three sections, making six braids. Each section was one big braid, except each braid looked like a huge S. It turned out to be the same exact hairstyle I saw years later in the movie *Baby Boy*, in the scene when Tyrese's character, Jodi, and his homeboy whipped on the teenage gang-banger with a belt instead of knocking him out for stealing his bike in front of the liquor store.

I realized when I was braiding 8Ball that I couldn't allow people to sit between my legs the way I used to do on the porch as a kid. If I wanted to consider myself a professional, I needed to use chairs instead. So 8Ball was the last person I braided in that position.

Not long after I braided 8Ball, my confidence grew, and I was braiding the locals as if I were an artist painting a picture. My dad had been a popular African American artist, especially in the seventies, and he must've passed down some of his artistic talent to me—except my canvas was one's head.

Terrence, aka Pusha T, was my first rapper client to ever go onstage directly after I'd braided him. He was part of the rap duo Clipse, along with his brother, Malice. They were from Virginia Beach and produced by Pharrell Williams, who was one half of the duo The Neptunes. I met Pusha T at his room at the Hyatt Place Hotel in Buckhead, but for some reason, I just couldn't get the parts in his head right. I knew they were crooked, and I let him go onstage in front of thousands of people with his head jacked up. I didn't get to actually see the show and secretly prayed that he'd worn a baseball cap of some sort. To my surprise, he still called me for another appointment. This time I met him at his Colony Square Hotel room in midtown, and I totally redeemed myself.

Not all my styles were turning out great, but I was getting much better. I did learn that, just like in corporate America, I had my good and bad days, regardless of my profession.

Not too long after adding Pusha T to my client list, I met up with one of my Georgia State alumni buddies, AD, at the Pink Pony Strip Club on Buford Highway to shoot pool and have a couple of drinks. We happened to be sitting across from a guy whose braids looked really rough, as if they hadn't been done in months. His head was so frizzy that it looked like an Afro with braids somewhere underneath it. It was Andre Rison, the ex–Atlanta Falcon wide receiver. I knew he really needed my help, so I went into braider mode and gave him my card. But it wasn't just that his hair desperately needed my attention. This was *the* Andre Rison, ex–Atlanta Falcon number 85, and he had to have a pot of gold hidden somewhere. If my memory served me correctly, he was one of the most paid receivers in the NFL at one time. Then again, I probably only gave him his props because he was the ex-boyfriend of Lisa "Left Eye" Lopes of the group TLC. I loved those girls.

When I approached Andre and offered my services, he put me on the spot, as if he didn't believe I could braid. I took it like he was saying that I wasn't black or ethnic enough. So I pulled out a hair comb and started to take his braids down one by one, right there at the club while folks watched, and rebraid them.

My gullible ass. He didn't break me off with any loot—not even ten dollars! I got absolutely nada for putting my hands in his dirty hair that night. But he did promise that if I came by his place the following week, I would be paid for the second braiding session as well as the first.

A week later, I drove the thirty-plus miles to Stone Mountain and ended up on a cute little cul-de-sac in a community where all the homes resembled one another, with their solid colors, single chimneys, garage fronts and all-vinyl siding.

The house I pulled up in front of was three stories high and had maybe four bedrooms. After I parked my

4Runner in front of the home, Andre directed me to the back of the house from the top of the stairs so I could enter through the basement. Once inside, I seemed to be in some type of musical artist's home, and I could tell it definitely wasn't Andre's home because it seemed too girly. I was like, "Damn, why doesn't he want to get his hair done at his own house?" Then I thought, "Oh yeah, Left Eye burned it down."

On the left was an office/studio that was separated by half wall and half glass. On the walls were several of TLC's music award plaques from the American Music Awards, MTV, and Billboard. The office looked like it could have doubled as a recording studio: I saw a microphone, keyboards, and sound machines. Andre had a few homeboys in the basement chilling; they were seated on a sectional couch just to the right of the office, watching a Monday Night Football game on a sixty-inch floor-model television.

In front of the sofa stood a black wrought-iron spiral staircase that I could tell had to be a renovation that connected the kitchen and basement. The steps were so shaky as I walked up them and into the kitchen area that I thought I was going to break my neck. The kitchen table and chairs and were very art deco, but there was nothing that stood out that made me believe Left Eye was a real superstar. For example, some of the singers' and stars' homes in Hollywood were way fancier. Lisa's home seemed like the average Joe's, and I liked that. It made me believe she could have been a down-to-earth person. On my way to the guest bathroom, I noticed a customized black-and-white floor rug with a musical note on it. I thought that was so cool.

Andre eventually told me that this was Left Eye's spot, but she was out of the country and he didn't know when she would be back. He said they were still cool friends regardless of their past. After braiding his head, I left.

Less than two weeks later, he summoned me for yet another appointment. This time we met at another house, not too far from Left Eye's. This house also had a music studio, one that looked more professional. It was soundproof, and the recording room was stand-alone. Glass separated the vocalist from the production-equipment table.

This time he and I were alone, and the more Andre and I talked, the more he began to tell me about himself and his musical interests. Apparently, football was a thing of the past. Music was his interest now. He told me he was partly responsible for TLC's song "Waterfalls." I wasn't sure if there was any truth to what he was saying because no members of TLC were there to dispute it. Besides, Andre didn't strike me as a musician, at least not until he let me listen to a couple of songs he'd created while working on his first CD, which he said would be released later that year. I was convinced then that there could be some truth in what he said, especially by the way he handled the production equipment.

I wasn't around Andre in the early nineties when he supposedly ran Atlanta. But when I first came to Atlanta, I heard stories about Andre and his buddy Tupac and how they were larger than life back then. Now, Andre seemed like a really low-key kind of guy.

After I'd been braiding Andre for a couple of months, we began kicking it. Occasionally I would fire up a blunt or two, and we'd smoke together. For some reason, after one of those sessions, we started to make out. Maybe it was the cognac and the blunt. Our kissing led to sex, but only because I wanted to say that I'd had sex with Left Eye's old boyfriend.

After our first sexual encounter, I noticed a slight increase in his appointments, from twice a month to almost weekly. He wanted to see me sooner than every two weeks, he said. At this point, Andre and I talked often, and he told me many stories about playing for the Atlanta Falcons, hanging with Tupac Shakur, and his and Lisa's love/hate relationship. I found him credible and interesting.

After a few months of braiding, smoking blunts, and having sex, the relationship ran its course. Apparently, while he worked on his upcoming CD, he had a new interest, in the form of the new young female backup singer who was working with him on a song. He said that she had been recommended for his upcoming CD. She was cute but appeared to be more than a backup singer. All of a sudden, I felt like a third wheel. I decided to not take his calls anymore and swallowed the fact that I shouldn't have had to compete with a Janelle Monáe look-alike for his attention anyway.

Was It Because I Swallowed

CHAPTER 11

Left Eye wasn't the only member of TLC whose man wore braids. T-Boz's husband at the time, rapper MACK 10, became a client of mine as well. I met MACK at the Shark Bar Restaurant that used to be on Peachtree Street, not far from North Avenue.

MACK was seated at the head of a huge table with a party of at least a dozen people when I managed to give him my card. He took it and promised to call me to schedule an appointment. The following week he asked me to meet him in the Suwanee area at The Reserve at Sugarloaf Apartments, directly across from the subdivision where he shared a home with his then wife, T-Boz. I asked my friends Brandy and Angel to come with me because they wanted to meet him, too.

MACK was from Los Angeles, and having lived there myself, I felt he and I had that West Coast connection going on, except he didn't smoke weed. I found that out after my girls rolled up and he said that wasn't for him. It was OK. I couldn't smoke and braid at the same time anyway, or else I'd lose focus.

I began my usual process of washing, conditioning, and blow-drying. But MACK was different from all of my other clients because his hair was three times as long and very thick, and he was insanely tender headed. He looked like he wanted to knock me out after I'd finished blow-drying his head.

Even after a few sessions, the process never got easier. The more I braided him, the more he reminded me of my kid customers, who often can't sit still during the braiding process.

Even though MACK had a regular braider in Los Angeles, he allowed me to get in where I fit in. He was cool, even though after the third time, he asked if I wouldn't mind braiding him in my bra and panties. I chose not to, but I did undress and model for him to show him how banging my body was. I was confident. I just couldn't understand why he would want anything other than his superstar wife, T-Boz. She was talented, beautiful, and a great catch for any man.

I had much respect for T-Boz and wouldn't dare disrespect her family, even if he tried to pay me for it. I kinda respected Left Eye, too, and only got with Andre because I really thought Left Eye didn't want him anymore, and I didn't mind taking her leftovers.

The braiding business was going well with the rappers, but I was always looking to take on new clients from all the different industries.

My very first pro-athlete customer was a NBA rookie named DJ. DJ was a shooting guard with the Atlanta Hawks. He was six foot nine, barely 200 pounds soaking wet, and only twenty years old when we met. I approached him in the VIP section of a club in Buckhead. He had twists in his hair at the time and said he was thinking about locking them up. I was able to convince him that his twists were long enough for me to braid instead. I explained all of my hair services and hair products and even told him about my door-to-door service.

At the time, DJ lived only minutes away from the club, so it was easy for him to direct me to his apartment at the Barclay on Piedmont in Buckhead.

The following day I braided DJ's hair. Afterward we ended up going out drinking and then had sex, which I realized was not a good business practice. I had to swallow that mistake. I blamed it on the alcohol; still, it never should've happened. DJ was too young and immature for me. I believe he was one of those rookies on a pussy rampage, sexing up anything that would give him the green light.

I was able to fix that situation by apologizing for my unprofessional behavior. I told him that it would never happen again. I used the old Jedi mind trick, and it worked. I'm glad it did, because one Atlanta Hawk customer turned into another and, over the next few years, into several NBA players.

Ean was a potential new player for the Atlanta Hawks and was referred to me by DJ.

When Ean summoned me to his hotel room at the Embassy Suites in downtown Atlanta, I could hear the cash register ringing in my head.

When he opened the door, I thought I'd died and gone to heaven. He was the finest light-skinned man I'd ever seen. In the doorway stood this handsome brother who was six foot seven and over 220 pounds with hazel eyes and naturally tinted blond hair. GQ magazine should have let him grace its cover, he was so fine. His smile made me want to give him unlimited free hairdos. I had to catch myself because my rent needed to be paid. When he spoke, it took a few moments before I could process what he was saying and respond because he was so fucking fine.

As I began my usual hair-braiding process along with the typical get-acquainted conversation, I couldn't help but smell his aura. I could tell he still had a hood side to him even though he was in the league.

Ean began to tell me that he was trying out for the Hawks, but I could sense that he was unsure whether he'd made the team. All I knew was that sadness was written all over his face, and I wanted nothing more than to make his day end on a high note.

His lips were so pink and puffy that I had to touch them, so I kissed him. When I did, his penis began to swell. As he sat on the bed, I sat in his lap, hoping he'd fall back and let me have my way with him. And he did. After he strapped up, I sat on him and got busy. At that point, I had made it a rule to always use condoms because I was doing a lot of spontaneous fucking and didn't want to catch any diseases.

I whispered in his ear, "Whatever is eating at you, let it go." While riding him, I messed up his new hairdo. It didn't matter. I told myself I would gladly rebraid it again tomorrow. But when tomorrow came, he was gone.

He hadn't made the team and was sent back to Michigan. But that wouldn't be the end of my braiding Ean's hair. Weeks later, he called me to let me know he was back in Atlanta. They had called him back, decided to give him another shot, and he had finalized a contract with the Hawks as a power forward. "What a relief," I thought. I wasn't ready to be done with his fine ass.

Upon his return to Atlanta, I braided Ean regularly for two seasons at either his rented midtown apartment or the brand-new townhome he purchased in Buckhead. And 80 percent of the time, those braiding sessions always ended with us getting it on.

The following NBA season, DJ left the Hawks, and Ean remained my only Hawk customer that year until he was traded to the Cleveland Cavaliers.

After he relocated to Cleveland, I managed to continue to braid his hair, and he even referred Anderson

Varejao, a center for the Cavaliers, who spoke very little English.

I didn't like flying to Cleveland because the weather sucked whenever I flew in to braid. But I got both money and sex for my braid services, so I figured I more than broke even. I would've followed Ean to East Japeepee if he wanted me to. However, once he was traded to the Los Angeles Lakers, I stopped hearing from him altogether. To this day I've swallowed the hurt of him not calling me, if only to say he'd found another braider.

Was It Because I Swallowed

CHAPTER 12

I was really getting the hang of my new chosen profession, even with its unpredictable schedule. I would get calls throughout the day and sometimes at all hours of the night. I was less concerned about what time the calls came in and more concerned with how much I would be paid. The crazier the hour, the more I charged. Most times, for late-night calls, I would leave with at least a C-note or more per head. That's one hundred dollars, if you didn't know.

I was enjoying what I did, and my clients were happy, too, because they had healthy hair, neat designs, and me as their braider. It was all the proof I needed that I had made the right decision. I no longer wished to go back into a corporate environment.

My life was devoid of stress and the pressure of being on the clock. I was even more grateful to be relieved of my superiors with their up-and-down personalities and office politics.

I didn't think braiding was the ideal job for someone who had put forth the dedication, time, and effort to earn a degree, but as long as it paid the bills and I had the freedom to keep my own schedule, I was good.

For the locals I started charging fifty dollars for men, because some guys I'd met had started growing hair just so that they could sit in my chair and get braided by me.

The prices for pro athletes and artists varied, depending on where I had to travel to and at what time of the day. Prices for kids and females ranged from thirty to seventy dollars. Even if I added extensions, I tried to look out for my hardworking black sistas.

I wouldn't have been able to look out for any of my clients if I hadn't been able to secure a top-ten NBA player named JoJo. JoJo was dark skinned, six foot eleven, 250 pounds, and only twenty-two years old.

I caught him just as he was about to jump into his candy-apple-red convertible Bentley in front of the Magic City Strip Club in downtown Atlanta. He was pulling off in a rush somewhere, but I yelled out to him anyway. As I quickly ran toward him and his shiny new whip, I introduced myself, handed him my card, and told him I was the braider DJ had recently referred to him.

JoJo took my card with a smile and said he'd be calling me from a 317 area code and to make sure I answered. He said it with authority—like he was the boss, and I was ready to take orders.

A few days later, JoJo gave me directions to his apartment in Buckhead. It was a two-bedroom, two-bath apartment in the Estates at Phipps behind Phipps Plaza off Lenox Road. By this time, I traveled with my hair products in a durable blue Tupperware bin with a handle in the center. People would often mistake me for a cleaning lady or something.

I knocked on his door, and one of his homeboys let me in. I waited for him to enter the kitchen, which seemed the logical place to do his hair. When JoJo stepped out of the bedroom toward me, I thought he was going to have to duck through the threshold of the doorway because he was so tall. He looked way finer than he had the night we first met. His now clearly visible dark, baby-smooth skin and nice facial features threw me off. I remember catching a chill. I was like, "Damn! What have we here?"

He and I exchanged greetings, and I recommended that he sit at the kitchen table so that I could begin to take his braids down. I politely asked him if we were on any set schedule; I wanted to be sure to take my time.

As I started taking his braids down one by one, I couldn't help but to smell JoJo, and he smelled so good. I could tell he had just gotten out of the shower. His energy was great, and I was already enjoying being in his presence. Wow! I couldn't help but thank God to be in that apartment with that young millionaire, up close and personal, and be compensated for it. It didn't get any better than that.

I started to talk a little to break the ice. As I spoke, JoJo's houseguest disappeared into the second bedroom, slowly closing the door. I continued talking about the weather and world issues because JoJo seemed a little shy and reserved at first. By the time his braids were out, I had told him a little about myself and had gone down the list of other professionals I'd already braided. JoJo eventually told me he was originally from Columbia, South Carolina, but lived and played pro basketball in Indianapolis, Indiana.

Things were going smoothly with JoJo, and our conversation was only getting better. I washed and blow-dried his hair, and then he received a call from his daughter's mother. She ended up staying on the phone with him until I was down to the last couple of braids. By that time, whatever connection we had seemed broken. The only thing that needed to be discussed was payment for my services.

JoJo gave me $200 and told me he'd call me again soon. I got excited, telling myself there was more money where that came from. But I knew I had to take it one step at a time and secure him as a returning client first, so I thanked him for the opportunity and left.

During our second appointment less than two weeks later, JoJo seemed a little friendlier and more engaged. The more we talked, the more genuine he seemed. He was funny, open-minded, and mature for his age. I was really digging him, and I knew he could tell because he flirted back. I told him about my family upbringing, education, and traveling experiences. We talked about his buddy, DJ, and how they met. We even talked about the club hot spots and popular events happening. I enjoyed his company, and he seemed to get all of my jokes. I was digging that.

After the first two appointments, our professional relationship as stylist and client fell to the wayside. He looked like an NBA poster boy. He was so dark and so tall with an impossibly handsome boyish face. When I looked into his dark eyes, he seemed to have all the answers to my financial prayers. I couldn't help myself. I had to jump his bones.

As I was bending over to pack up my hair products, I turned around to see JoJo sitting on his bed, staring at me as if to say, "You know you want this." He didn't have to say a word because our chemistry said it all. I wanted to fuck JoJo so bad that I was breathless. I walked in his room, closed the door, and began to feast on his baby-soft skin.

At first he was a little shy, but I didn't care and led the way by taking his shirt off so that I could kiss and lick his smooth and hairless chest. I couldn't keep my hands off him. While I licked and kissed, I went for his zipper so that his soldier could come out to play. I wanted him in my mouth so bad but couldn't—at least not that soon. I made him stand up and pulled his shorts down. I pushed him back onto the bed and continued to feast because I couldn't help myself. Surprisingly, he didn't taste like chocolate as I'd imagined he would. Instead, he tasted innocent and pure, as if he was inexperienced and had never been touched the way I was touching him.

We started over again because our first time was so much fun. I really enjoyed our exchanges. Over the years, it seemed the more I sexed JoJo, the more money he gave me, more than any other celebrity acquaintance of mine.

After the first couple of months, JoJo's braids came with optional blow jobs. Unless we were in Indianapolis at the home he shared with his daughter's mother, that is.

I knew he had a girlfriend, but frankly I didn't give a damn. Apparently, he didn't either because he continued to send for me every ten days. He only paid for me to fly coach, but I didn't mind because I got to travel on his tab. It didn't take long for me to be on a first-name basis with his personal travel agent either.

Whenever I landed at the airport, he was there to pick me up in a different luxury car from his fleet, which included a Ferrari, a G500 Mercedes wagon, a BMW X5, and a 645 convertible BMW.

JoJo's beautiful and insanely expensive home was only a fifteen-minute drive from the airport and was surrounded by eight-foot-high iron gates that could be entered only by keypad or with an automatic gate opener. As we pulled onto his property, we had to drive around to the back of the house to park. On the left side of his home was a separate in-law suite on top of a multicar garage with carriage-house doors. To the right was the back entrance of the main house.

When we entered through the kitchen, JoJo demanded that I take off my shoes; it was the house rule.

The house was empty because JoJo's girlfriend was picking up their daughter from preschool.

The kitchen looked like a Martha Stewart gourmet kitchen with its top-of-the-line appliances and oversized refrigerator. The cabinets were handcrafted distressed white oak under granite countertops. There was even an island in the center with a built-in sink and wine cooler.

The sunken living room was directly in front of the kitchen. The living area had floor-to-ceiling windows, a vaulted ceiling, and a huge fireplace. The white mantel above displayed several framed family pictures. These huge pictures were of him, his baby's mom, and their toddler daughter. To the right of the living room stood another living area with an entrance to a foyer that was completely covered in marble tile.

Once I got to the foyer, I could see the upstairs bedroom doors through the highly crafted banisters that traveled from the bottom step up the stairwell.

As JoJo disappeared, I took it upon myself to tour parts of his home. The door was open, so I walked downstairs and into the basement. There were framed awards and sports memorabilia on the walls, a fully loaded bar, a Brunswick pool table, and even a high-tech movie theater.

As I walked back upstairs to the kitchen, his girlfriend and their daughter were walking through the door.

JoJo looked at me crazy. I could tell in his mind he was like, "What the hell are you doing, Celeste?" JoJo finally said, "Celeste, this is Mela, and that's my daughter."

Mela, who was light skinned with long hair, was really cute and had a warm smile. Their daughter, who was only five years old, looked just like JoJo, except she was much cuter, caramel in color, and really tall for her age.

After small talk with Mela, I liked her instantly. There was a great energy about her, and she seemed really down-to-earth. She was a twenty-two-year-old twin, originally from Oregon. "How cool is that to have a twin," I thought. Mela was so supercool that my conscience began bugging me.

You see, I'm sure Mela didn't have any idea about my relationship with JoJo. I just needed to swallow any guilty feelings I had. "It takes two to tango," I told myself, making me only halfway wrong.

After I'd finished JoJo's hair, I packed up, told everyone it was a pleasure meeting them, and said good-bye until next time. JoJo then drove me back to the airport.

For almost an entire season, I flew into Indianapolis in snow, sleet, and rain. It was all worth it because the pay was always $400 or $500.

In fact, the only issue I had with traveling to braid JoJo that season was that I couldn't have sex with him when I saw him. I was afraid that we would be caught in the act. I respected Mela enough that I didn't show any type of emotions toward him or touch him in a way that would make her think anything was going on.

JoJo was my most important client and a major factor in my life. My regular customers would get upset when I went out of town to do his hair, but that didn't matter to me because they couldn't pay me a fraction of what he could for a day's work. Nor could my regular customers get me a shout-out on national television.

During a flight to Indianapolis to braid JoJo, I befriended an associate of Bill Walton's who was an executive for Rolls Royce. Bill Walton was a sportscaster, and during an Indiana Pacers home game, he told the audience, "I hear Celeste, JoJo's braider, is in town, and I was told that she is a looker."

My phone was ringing off the hook with people calling me, including the ex–NBA player Walt, to tell me this, and I wasn't even seated in the audience to be pointed out. I couldn't believe I'd missed my five minutes of fame.

After my second NBA season with JoJo, he relocated his kicking-it spot from Atlanta to South Beach, Miami. Yea! I was geeked about that because now he would be farther from Mela's jurisdiction.

The moment I stepped outside the Miami airport, JoJo was there to pick me up in a stretch limo to take us to our beach-front hotel. This was only my second time visiting Miami. The weather was awesome, the beaches were everywhere, and the sun-tanned people were beautiful. It reminded me much of Los Angeles with all the sun, ocean, and palm trees.

After arriving at the Lowe's Hotel on South Beach, JoJo told me what room he'd be in, handed me my room key, and headed up to his room. I took the elevator up to my room and dropped my bags off. I was crazy excited. Finally, I could be alone with JoJo after flying into Indianapolis all winter long and not being able to touch him the way I wanted to. I'd developed a craving for pleasing him. Now the torture had ended.

I started to fast-walk down to JoJo's room. I couldn't get there quick enough. I couldn't wait to talk to him alone, to be in his space and breathe him in.

When I got to his room, I expected spur-of-the-moment, steamy sex before our braid session. Instead he was standing at the sink, eager for me to start the hair process. "OK, we're going to stick to the old routine and get busy afterward," I thought. But when I finished, he jumped up and headed toward the bathroom to take a shower. I couldn't understand why he didn't want to jump my bones the way I did his.

He kept walking toward the shower, only slowing to tell me to enjoy the rest of the day in the sun, as if he had other plans or something. Even after telling him I hadn't brought a bathing suit to enjoy the beach, he shouted, "Go ahead and get one from the hotel boutique, and charge it to your room." I lowered my head like a cupid missing the target with the last bow and thanked him for inviting me to Miami. I went back to my room feeling like a failure.

Later that evening he called me to come to his room; I knew it was going down once I saw him. I'd waited almost an entire basketball season to crawl up and down his long body. All I wanted to do was take my time and make slow, passionate love to my NBA poster boy, kiss him lovingly, and show him how much I'd truly missed him. Not JoJo—his ass just wanted to fuck.

He wasn't trying to be all lovey-dovey. I figured that was because he was probably doing the lovey-dovey thing with Mela. It didn't bother me at first because Mela was my only competition. At least I thought she was, until I visited him a few more times in Miami and found out there were other chicks he was fucking around with.

Was It Because I Swallowed

CHAPTER 13

After a month or so of my flying into Miami to braid JoJo, he decided to lease a high-rise condominium. The lobby door of the new building opened up onto Ocean Drive and restaurant row. The beach-front condominium was a two-bedroom, two-bath with all the amenities. The high-tech kitchen had a wine cooler, and each room had a balcony and walk-in closets. The balconies really took the cake because they offered an endless view of the ocean and South Beach's boardwalk just below.

During one of my visits, I arrived at JoJo's condo early one Saturday morning from the Miami airport and noticed a dark-colored Mercedes G500 wagon outside. I stepped out of the cab with my products in hand, ready to rock 'n' roll on JoJo's hair, and I approached the concierge to have him notify JoJo of my arrival. Waiting, I noticed a black chick pacing back and forth by the lobby doors; she appeared to be calling someone on her cell phone. She looked pissed.

When I got upstairs, I asked JoJo if he was expecting anyone.

"Yep," he said. "Sabrina," the female rapper.

"Oh, so that's who that was?" I said.

Just then I heard noise coming from his bedroom. I couldn't believe his ass. JoJo already had company, he had Sabrina downstairs in the lobby trying to come up, and then there was me in the middle of all of that. I gave him a look like, "What do you want me to do?"

"Just leave me alone for a couple of hours. I just got in from the club, and I need some sleep," he said.

I must have been a fool to think that Mela was my only competition. The reality was that in Miami he was probably getting more pussy thrown at him than in Atlanta. From the looks of things, he was catching it, too. I just brushed it off and left to go eat breakfast until he was ready.

As JoJo's official braider, I had to play my position. I felt obligated to do just that because I could lose the first-class treatment at clubs and restaurants and the cash that came along with my assigned title. There were moments when I felt unsure of which role I was to play. Was I his employee or his lover? It all began to take its toll on me, even though I never let him know it.

Once I drove two hours east of Atlanta to JoJo's hometown of Columbia, South Carolina, to service him. This time we shared a room at the St. Mark Hotel in the downtown area. My plan was to arrive late Friday afternoon in order to enjoy the rest of the evening and return the following day. Everything went as planned because I was done with his head that night by nine and dressed by ten to hang out.

I went downstairs to the restaurant where JoJo and his homeboy were already enjoying food and drinks. While eating, JoJo said that he would be hosting a party the following night at a nightclub that was on the other side of the restaurant. He mentioned a couple of other people that were hosting, including LisaRaye. That sounded like it was going to be hot. I wanted to be there for that.

I asked JoJo why he didn't tell me about it before I left Atlanta. "If you had told me, I would have brought an extra outfit for the event."

I was rocking a really nice two-piece cropped jean pantsuit with some hot jean high-heeled knee boots. If I had known about the party or LisaRaye, I would've waited to wear what I already had on. I asked JoJo if I could have some money to go to the mall the next day for an outfit. He laughed and said no. He obviously thought something was funny or that, I was somehow intimidated by LisaRaye. It wasn't that at all. I just wasn't prepared. I like to think that I was a boss bitch myself, and, being that, I wouldn't dare show up to a ball without the right gown or slippers. So I went back to the Atlanta with my head down, feeling like a Cinderella that had missed the ball.

After a while, I got confused about what JoJo really wanted from me. Was it physical, emotional, or just professional? I figured maybe if I studied JoJo's relationship with his daughter's mother, it would help me to define mine with him.

One day, during the following basketball season, while waiting for him to get out of the shower, I asked Mela how she dealt with JoJo and his high-profile lifestyle. I wanted to know what it was like to be the number one female in his life.

She said their relationship wasn't perfect and that they'd been together since she was a senior in high school. JoJo was all she knew. They occasionally had minor issues here and there with other women, but it wasn't anything she couldn't handle.

Unbeknownst to her, I was one of those females. At that moment, I didn't see anything wrong with sitting across the table from her with a straight face because I had my own agenda. That's not to say I didn't swallow the wrong of it all—I did. I wanted to apologize, but it was hard because I couldn't see past the checks JoJo was writing me.

After years of being with JoJo, I simply learned to play my position and do as he told me. I wouldn't dare question anything he told me to do, not even bringing him the baddest chick in a club to please him for the night if he requested it.

I knew JoJo loved that I was down for almost whatever. I made no secret of that; in fact, I made a point of reminding him whenever I could. Shit, JoJo's young millionaire ass could do whatever the fuck he wanted. In order to stay on his team, I knew I had to give him what he wanted, or some other bitch would. That was my biggest fear.

It wasn't until after my third NBA season of braiding JoJo that my fear came true. I could no longer stand on the sidelines when he started to fuck with multiple bitches openly, right in front of my face.

I was glad to be on JoJo's team, but I had to swallow the regret of ever having crossed the line.

Was It Because I Swallowed

CHAPTER 14

Over the years that I traveled back and forth as JoJo's braider, I continued to braid other pro athletes as well. By then my local celebrity clientele in Atlanta had grown considerably. I was doing my thing, and my name was out there as a recommended braider among all ballers. Celebrity or not, my braids were popular.

There was one celebrity that I would've done anything to get at, even though he didn't always wear braids. I was plotting, even trying to use other artists to figure out a way to meet the man in my ATLien dreams: André 3000, aka André Lauren Benjamin.

I would do just about anything to meet André. Let it be known that meeting him was one of the many reasons I moved to Atlanta in the first place.

I was grateful for black label executives. Back then, there were only a handful, like LA Reid of LaFace Records, who helped put Atlanta on the map with such artists as TLC and Toni Braxton. But Outkast had something different about them. Their original mix of rap mixed with a bit of instrumental funk was brilliant.

Some songs on their debut album, like "Funky Ride," reminded me of my mom's seventies Parliament Funkadelic and eighties Con Funk Shun albums. My favorite song on Outkast's first album was "Git Up, Git Out." I told myself if ever given the opportunity, I would sing André his whole verse. I was really crazy about him. The energy that came through his music videos made me just want to reach out and touch him.

I almost did, too, when I ran into local talents Rico Wade and Khujo on separate occasions. They were both members of the Atlanta Dungeon Family, who I thought was an arm's length away from André.

Rico was a producer who ran Organized Noize, and Khujo was with the rap group Goodie Mob. The Dungeon Family also consisted of two other talents, Joi and OutKast, one of my favorite rap duos.

Khujo was in his early twenties. He was brown skinned with braids and very mysterious. I thought he had a dark side. Even my neighbors picked up on it. They were concerned on the few occasions he pulled up to my apartment in his 1970s Ford Galaxie, wearing a long, dark trench coat, sometimes brandishing a machete. But I knew he was harmless.

Unfortunately, Khujo and I did cross that line once and have sex. Afterward I had to swallow the fact that I'd just had sex with a man who was brandishing a sword of some type—and that I was completely cool with that.

Shortly after running into Khujo, I met Rico Wade, a producer from the *Southernplayalisticcadillacmuzik* CD, who was also instrumental in Outkast's and Goodie Mob's success. That debut album went platinum and secured the number-twenty spot on Billboard's Top 200, it was so hot.

Rico was dark skinned, 170 pounds, and barely six feet tall with a warm smile that often spread across his narrow face.

I was fairly fond of him, maybe because within only minutes of our first conversation, he offered me four tickets to Puffy's All White Linen Party at the Fox Theatre in 1998. Say no more. Rico had my attention, especially if he could get me more free entertainment tickets.

The only catch for Puffy's party passes was that I had to drive all the way to Rico's house off Cascade Road, the same exit as Too Short's, and pick them up. Once I arrived at his white plantation-style house with its porch and columns—and before he handed the tickets over—Rico invited me in to give me a tour. He said it housed the original Dungeon Family recording studio. "No way!" I thought. I was thrilled and couldn't help but give him two thumbs up for living where Outkast's magical debut album had been made. I couldn't believe that I was going to be able to enter that very same studio.

To my surprise it was the smallest recording space I'd ever seen. It had foam-padded cushions stapled to some of the walls. I could only conclude that they served as makeshift soundproofing or something. It was awkwardly shaped, and all the walls were black, which made it appear even smaller. I'd visited a few music studios in Atlanta, and in comparison this one was tiny. None of that mattered because I was proud to be standing next to a pioneer in music production. I had to give Rico his props.

As we walked out of his home and toward the car, I wanted to slip in a question or two about André, but the conversation somehow always ended up back on Rico and Organized Noize, instead. But that was OK, too.

But, I considered, this was my second failed attempt to get next to my down-South man, André. I fucked up the first by sleeping with Khujo.

I thanked Rico, drove off, and headed home to get ready for an evening of fun. I called my homegirls, and within two hours Nakia, Lydia, and Erika were at my apartment just a few blocks from the Fox Theatre.

In our white and off-white painted-on dresses with matching pumps and purses, we all piled into my ride. You couldn't tell us nothing!

Everyone at the party was looking sexy or handsome, dressed in all white or off-white attire. We had a fantastic time, and to this day, I am thankful to Rico for passing on those tickets to me.

A couple of years after meeting Rico and just after I started braiding, I met Robert Barnett, aka T-Mo of Goodie Mob. I didn't see it as a coincidence that he had hair down to his back. T-Mo was the cutest of the Goodie Mob family with his caramel-colored skin and nice facial features. He became my first Dungeon Family braid customer.

T-Mo came into my braid shop on Candler Road on a visit to the tint shop next door. I was happy he did. I stayed on deck for more music industry clients just like him.

At the beginning of our braid session, I told T-Mo that I had already befriended Khujo and Rico, hoping to make him feel more comfortable talking to me. At that time, T-Mo was expecting his first child with his longtime girlfriend, whom he said he'd grown up with. T-Mo seemed easygoing even though he didn't talk too much.

Too bad his hair wasn't as easygoing. Instead it was really thick, long, and unmanageable. It was a challenge to do, as if each strand had it out for me: they refused to cooperate. I knew I was hurting him. As I combed and blow-dried his hair, he squirmed, grunted, and groaned.

I figured I'd never see him again. But a few weeks later, I was glad to see that he'd returned, giving me another chance to possibly become his regular braider.

During this braid session, I tried to use some tact by waiting to pop the "Where's André?" question. I didn't want to seem like a groupie the second time I braided his head. After all, steady clientele was more important.

After holding it for the entire braid session, at the end, I busted out and said, "Do you know whether or not André is in town?"

I think I caught him off guard. He looked at me, startled, as if I had turned into a crazy groupie right in front of his eyes. But Operation André failed: T-Mo said he hadn't seen or heard from André in months.

The only information I did get in later braid sessions from T-Mo was a little civil rights history. It turned out that T-Mo's family owned and operated Barnett's Café on Martin Luther King Boulevard, over by Morris Brown, Morehouse, and Spelman Colleges. His family had owned the business since the fifties or sixties, around the civil rights era, and many of those involved in the peaceful protests had eaten there. I was glad to have had the chance to eat some good breakfast there shortly before it closed its doors in the late nineties, and I was grateful to have made the connection between him and his family business, but it got me no closer to meeting André.

Shortly after I braided T-Mo, another Goodie Mob member, Cameron Gipp, aka Big Gipp, was referred to me for braids as well. The couple of braiding sessions I had with Big Gipp yielded nothing on André, so I decided to leave the subject alone altogether and almost gave up.

I must have been doing something wrong to manage to come in contact with a majority of the Dungeon Family but not the group's leader.

I even ran into Big Boi, the other half of Outkast, at the Gentlemen's Strip Club, but for some reason I wasn't interested in using him to get to André, even when my homegirl Erica told me Big Boi had asked for my number. I turned him down because everyone knew it was taboo to kick it with more than one person in a group, and I was saving myself for the big fish.

Finally, out of nowhere, I was personally invited by my homegirl Adrene to Outkast's first fashion show featuring their new clothing line. It was being hosted at Keith Sweat's old nightclub, The Industry, on Cheshire Bridge in the Buckhead area.

Adrene herself had transitioned from corporate America into wholesale retail. She knew what she wanted, then went after it. Adrene was a mix of Spanish and black and too beautiful with her smooth, silky brown skin and pretty facial features. She was a fashion diva who sometimes looked like a real-life Barbie doll when made-up. Adrene was so into clothes and fashion that she turned her passion into a business and opened her own clothing store in East Atlanta called Pieces of Adrene.

I've always admired Adrene for that savvy business move she made back in 2000. She was such an inspiration, and she made my decision to transition from corporate America that much easier.

Adrene and I approached the club. The building was sophisticated, with its Spanish-style ceramic roof, twelve huge floating columns, and black railings that gave it a full porch view around one half of the exterior. It wasn't until we entered through the back door on the bottom level that I realized it had another level.

Inside was a small bar directly on the right, and in the center was a sunken dance floor with a disco ball hanging above it. There were two small VIP areas on each side of the dance floor, and as we walked farther in, I could see the DJ booth just opposite the entrance.

By the time we entered, the fashion show was already in progress upstairs in the lounge area. The T-shaped stage sat directly in the center of the lounge. Amateur fashion models were on the catwalk in Outkast's clothing line. The stage didn't look sturdy, and the models looked down at each step they took instead of striking a professional pose at the end of each strut.

The clothing line seemed mostly simple, basic cotton pieces, as if not much thought had gone into designing and producing them. I wasn't even upset that we were late for the show because the pieces I saw weren't all that to go in my wallet for.

It didn't appear that the crowd shared my opinion, though, because some of the pieces were selling. Not to mention everyone seemed to be enjoying the drinks and festivities and having a great time.

After chilling for a few minutes and surveying the area, I turned to my left and almost gagged. On the real, I almost fell out: there he was! Just like that, in the flesh! I couldn't believe that André 3000 was just a few feet away from me, within eyesight. Hell, within touch—if I could manage to find the courage to go over there.

I froze, trying to plan my next move. I didn't want to blow this, even though I was feeling very confident. I'd just had my hair highlighted with fresh blonde streaks, and I was looking quite fly. So, I took a deep breath, exhaled, then politely walked over. I handed André my card and introduced myself.

Was It Because I Swallowed

CHAPTER 15

I couldn't help feeling like Diana Ross in *Lady Sings the Blues* when Billie D. Williams reaches out to shake Diana's hand and introduces himself. It was as if when André spoke to me all I heard was Billie D. saying, "Well, are you gonna let my arm fall off?" It felt just like a dream.

For years I'd wished to meet André, and he was just as I'd imagined. His lips and eyes looked just the way they did in the music videos.

We talked for a couple of minutes about my services, but someone interrupted us, and he had to leave. He promised to call me later to talk more—about me, not my braiding. He said it just like that. I turned around like, "Yeah, baby!" I wanted to high-five someone, but no one was around. I couldn't believe that André was feeling me like I did him. After all these years, it felt awesome.

Just as he'd promised, the following night at two in the morning, André called, and I gladly answered. I cleared my throat, said hello, and pretended to still be awake, even though he had just woken me up from a deep sleep. I was so excited. I began to breathe so hard that I had to silently count to ten in order to slow my heart rate while listening to him speak.

André was in the studio, trying to finish his latest CD, *Speakerboxxx*, the music of which he said he just wasn't feeling anymore. He said that he and his music partner, Antwan "Big Boi" Patton, were moving in different directions.

He invited me to the studio that night, but I told him I don't do studios, especially at that time of night. It seemed too obvious that it could have been a booty call, and I knew I wanted more from André than just that.

Unlike other celebrities I'd fucked with, he meant something. I wanted to know everything about André, going back as far as his childhood. Surprisingly, André said it wasn't a problem that I couldn't come to the studio and continued to talk with me. Over the years I had done countless studio and hotel visits after midnight with everyone from pro athletes to musicians, and they had led to nothing but empty sex.

While on the phone with André, I could hear him in the background playing a banjo of some sort. He told me that he loved to learn to play new instruments and that he listened to a lot of jazz. He seemed like an old spirit to me, and I could tell that he was into quality and not quantity when it came to women, even before he told me so.

André seemed to respect my rejecting his studio invitation, unlike other musicians I'd encountered over the years. He also appeared fascinated by my wealth of knowledge and loved it when I introduced him to a couple of words he'd never heard before.

During that conversation, because it was so late, I told André that if he wasn't careful, I would come to him in succubus form even though we had yet to be intimate. I wasn't sure whether that was a good or bad thing because a succubus is a female demon said to seduce men while they sleep.

I know it may sound strange, but I knew that from that moment on, if André ever heard that word again, he'd think of me.

Eventually, I proved to be good company because after a couple of hours on the phone, he asked if he could see me sometime soon. "Of course," I replied. And for the next few days, whenever the phone rang, I was filled with anticipation that it was him on the other end.

He finally called, and we planned a date. André picked me up, and we visited my old rooftop at the Fulton Cotton Mills lofts for a spectacular view of Atlanta and more conversation. I really enjoyed conversing with André and looking into his eyes. They seemed to hold all the answers to the universe. And his lips were the perfect size. I wondered how soft they were.

I was so attracted to him. Not just physically, as I had been with all the other celebrities I'd encountered, but mentally as well. I think I really must've been maturing because I was attracted to a man's brain and not just his face and physique. Something about André's mind intrigued me. His conversation and his thoughts took me to a different level. Together we analyzed my braiding designs into an art form, and I was able to connect with him as an artist. He did say that when he was ready to get braided again, he would hit me up and give me a try. It was a good enough start for me, no matter where our friendship went.

As we continued our conversation, I got a call from my homegirl Kortni. She had a flat tire and was stuck a couple of miles away. The girl's timing was horrible, but I considered her my friend, so we went to her rescue.

André and I left the rooftop and jumped back in his new platinum Range Rover, listening to John Coltrane on the way. When we arrived at Kortni's car on 6th Street and Juniper in downtown Atlanta, Kortni was shell-shocked when she realized who had come with me to save her. To my surprise, André began to jack up her Nissan Altima and change the tire without even being asked.

While he changed Kortni's tire, out of nowhere came this crackhead-looking guy, trying to help out for spare change.

Only moments passed before the crackhead realized who André was. He frantically began to yell out across the block to all his crackhead buddies that André 3000 was over on his corner, changing a flat tire. Next thing we knew, about five zombielike people with dirty, ripped clothing were standing around André. It was like the "Thriller" video, staring André 3000 instead of Michael Jackson. It was hilarious! Finally, I had to tell them to step back until he was finished because André was insisting on changing the tire on his own.

After Kortni's tire was changed and she was good to go home, André drove me back to my place in Buckhead. We talked a little longer in his SUV, but that was the extent of it. André said that he had such a busy schedule that it would be hard to fit me in. After that unforgettable evening, he went to Los Angeles to take up acting classes, and I lost contact with him. I didn't blow up his phone because I figured if he wanted to talk to me again, he would call.

When I finally did try his number weeks later, it no longer worked. I had to swallow the disappointment and realize that he was way more focused on acting and making a name for himself in the movie industry than trying to start any kind of relationship with anyone, let alone me. He was chasing his dreams, and I told myself it would be smart of me to do the same.

Was It Because I Swallowed

CHAPTER 16

Even though I didn't get the chance to do André 3000's hair, braids were still popular across the country. All you had to do was check out a hip-hop video, TV show, or movie or almost any basketball game, football game, or boxing event—brothers were rocking braids more than ever.

I was getting so many referrals that I eventually had to rent another booth in a West End Atlanta beauty and barbershop just to keep up with the demand. In addition to referrals, I took walk-ins, but only if I was available.

I did it. I stepped out on faith and started my own business. It was a success, and I was totally committed and serious about every aspect of it. I was running it like the CEO of a Fortune 500 company, tackling every responsibility the business presented.

I had to balance my appointment schedule, purchase quality supplies and professional equipment such as dryers and irons, and still try to attend annual shows like the Bronner Brothers International Hair Show in order to stay on top of my braid game.

Bronner Brothers is an Atlanta-based company that was founded by Dr. Nathaniel H. Bronner in 1947. The company offered hair education and hair products and later published *Upscale* magazine. Every year for the last few decades, with the help of Dr. Bronner's six sons, Bronner Brothers has continued to offer hair battles. The company eventually moved the event from the Butler Street YMCA, just across from Grady Hospital, to the Georgia World Congress Center.

I needed to learn as much as possible about the hair game, considering I was now responsible for $125 per week in booth rent. Even on the days I didn't want to braid, I didn't have a choice because I was now obligated to pay operating expenses.

My earnings were becoming so consistent that I bought a Mercedes SUV and a condominium in the Old Fourth Ward area of Atlanta. I felt more confident about my hustle and knew it was only a matter of time before I got another client more famous and wealthier than JoJo. That is not to say that I didn't appreciate JoJo as a client. I will always be grateful for his business. Thanks to him, I was put on the map, and I made a lot of connections. But I still needed to expand my client list.

Since it was the era of black men rocking braids, I had the potential to get at hundreds of clients.

I had paid the price and learned my lesson about crossing the line and sleeping with clients. My goal became to keep it professional and get paid for my braid services and to not be identified as a groupie, gold digger, or loose chick in the hotel room when I was summoned by clients. I was focused more than ever on multiplying my A-list clientele and becoming even more successful at my craft. Any paid musician or athlete rocking braids I looked at now only as a potential braid client and nothing else.

My first Atlanta Falcon client was Elijah Williams, aka Eli. Eli was a cute dark-skinned brother who was five foot ten and just over 180 pounds.

I handed Eli my card while out one night in Buckhead, and he called me a few days later for an appointment. I met up with him at his apartment just north of the Atlanta downtown area.

Eli said he was from Florida and seemed to be a little on the quiet side. Even after I did my usual get-to-know-you conversation, he remained reserved. Our appointments thereafter didn't get much better because he just didn't talk much.

A couple of months into our braiding sessions, Eli got shot in the leg during an attempted robbery outside a local Atlanta nightclub. Amazingly, he was OK and maintained his same demeanor as if nothing had happened. He had a great poker face. I had hoped his injury wouldn't affect his performance on the football field, but it did. He was soon released from his team, and he moved back to Florida.

Lucky for me, there always seemed to be another pro athlete who needed his hair braided.

Kwame Brown, a nineteen-year-old rookie who was six foot eleven and close to 250 pounds, was a first-round draft pick for the Washington Wizards in 2001.

This was the same year Michael Jordan decided to come out of retirement and play for the Wizards, even donating his entire salary that year to the victims of 9/11. My hero!

During that time, the Washington Wizards were the second most watched NBA team ever. When Kwame opened the door of his Ritz Carlton Hotel room off Peachtree and Lenox Roads in Buckhead, he reminded me a lot of JoJo, with his dark, smooth skin and long arms and legs. The resemblance was so striking that immediately my body started to respond to him, but I knew I wasn't going to be barking up that tree again.

Besides, I wanted to see if I could get at Michael Jordan once my braid services were rendered. I didn't want to mess up that chance by stepping to Kwame.

After my usual get-to-know-you chat, sometime during the braiding process, I asked Kwame if we could visit his megasuperstar teammate Michael. Kwame politely told me that even as a teammate, he couldn't get at Michael like that outside of practice. I later read that Michael blamed the team for lacking focus that year, which caused them to miss the playoffs.

I braided Kwame that one time and am still unsure about who referred him. Other than that appointment, the only other time I saw him was when I ran into him once in Miami at Club Oasis. There in the club I wanted to ask him why he hadn't requested my services again, but I decided against it and swallowed the loss of his clientele instead.

Just like that, I could rebound with another NBA player, and I did. Mikki was light skinned, six foot eleven, and roughly 225 pounds. He played power forward for the Atlanta Hawks from 2002 to 2003. He was from South Carolina and was the coolest player in the NBA to me; not only did he drive a classic 1960s Thunderbird with suicide doors, but he also stayed in a penthouse apartment at 710 Peachtree Street.

A few celebrities had already lived at that address, including rapper Too Short. Mikki was later traded to the Seattle Supersonics, then to the Sacramento Kings, ultimately making it to the NBA Finals. I was happy for him. If anyone deserved a NBA Championship ring, it was this guy. Almost every time I finished braiding Mikki, we'd end up at somebody's strip club for the night.

Unfortunately, Mikki won the Worst Head of Hair award that year. His hair was so coarse and thick that it took three to sometimes four hours to do. Even though his hair was a nightmare, it was worth it because he was such a great client.

Over the years I managed to get at other Atlanta Hawk clients, such as TyTy, "Pig" Anderson, and even Joe Johnson's first cousin. However, TyTy would be my last client from the Atlanta Hawks. TyTy had a high-yellow skin tone and was about six feet tall and around 180 pounds. He was referred to me by Al Harrington, who used to play forward for the Indiana Pacers with JoJo but was later traded to the Atlanta Hawks. I braided TyTy for over two seasons, and, unfortunately, I made the same mistake with TyTy that I had with other NBA players. He and I became intimate after a session or two, just because I needed the money. After the exchange, I always felt like the loser in the equation. But I had to keep it moving.

As I continued to travel over the years for pleasure, I made a point of always bringing my braid supplies along just in case.

In Miami one year during the taping of the Video Music Awards, I ran into Joseph Cartagena, aka Fat Joe, who was leaving Club Oasis in South Beach. I introduced myself to him as JoJo's braider. Fat Joe was light skinned with a huge smile and a short wavy haircut. Although he was very chunky, he wasn't fat. I think they called him Fat Joe because he had a fat spirit. Something about his presence made him appear larger than life.

I liked him immediately, and after that introduction he made me feel as if I'd been made, the way the Mafia does when it receives its people with a huge embrace. I felt welcomed into his circle.

During our conversation, he asked if I could possibly braid his homeboy Benzino, a rapper and ex-CEO of *The Source* magazine, who was also in town to attend the taping of the award show. I told Fat Joe that I'd love to and gave him my card. The following day I met up with

Benzino in a restaurant he claimed to own that was under construction. Benzino, who was also light skinned, was five foot ten with fine, straight hair.

He pointed me toward a sink in the back of the kitchen that I should use to wash his hair. I didn't think it was sanitary because it was in the kitchen, so we found another one.

After the washing and drying process, I started to braid him. It became increasingly difficult because Benzino was very fidgety; he wouldn't stay still in the chair. I think he suffered from attention deficit disorder.

When I finished his hair, he paid me fifty dollars and asked if I was going to hang out after the filming of the awards.

"Not for fifty dollars," I thought to myself. I told him that I was on a flight back to Atlanta that evening and wouldn't be hanging out.

Benzino upped the ante by mentioning his suite at the Turnberry Isle Resort in Adventura. He said I could stay there if I wasn't ready to leave Miami just yet. He insisted that I go there and relax because he would be out for most of the night anyway. I told him I would, but only if there was an extra room and I could have my own space. Even if he didn't have the extra room, I knew I wouldn't turn the opportunity down because I remembered hearing and reading about this resort, the very place Whitney Houston had an altercation and video vixen turned author Karrine Stephans said she spent time with rapper Xhibit.

Trying not to seem too eager, I snatched his key card and took the fifty-dollar cab ride to the infamous resort. I had to see for myself what all the hype was about. I pictured a music artist's paradise.

It took less than thirty minutes to get there, but it looked way too secluded for being so close to Miami. There were palm trees everywhere, and it was so peaceful the minute I stepped out of the cab. Although it was eight on a Sunday, I was still expecting to see some activity, not the calm and serenity that was before me.

I opened the door to his hotel suite and walked in. The living area had a couch, chair, and coffee table and a flat-screen television inside an armoire. To the right was a closet that had a pullout bed. I guessed that was supposed to be the second bedroom Benzino had mentioned. The other room had a king-size bed as well as a huge bathroom on the opposite side. Inside the bathroom was a Jacuzzi and a huge window with a stunning view of the forest out back.

After taking a moment to let it all soak in, I wasted no time by running water for a bath to get started relaxing. While soaking I read a chapter from *Dreams Of My Father* by the then senator Barack Obama. I also took a moment to thank God for the opportunity to even be there.

After relaxing for at least an hour, I put on the white terrycloth robe that I found behind the bathroom door, cheerfully phoned the concierge, and ordered a cheeseburger, fries, and a Belvedere apple martini.

I couldn't have cared less about any award show. As a matter of fact, I never even turned the television on. I was just happy to have checked out of the Holiday Inn and into heaven on earth. After pulling down the bed, I fell asleep almost instantly.

Benzino returned around seven the next morning and jumped right into bed with me, even though there was a king-size bed in the other room. I was pissed: he'd told me he wanted nothing from me. And besides, I hadn't heard the shower running, and he smelled horrible.

I immediately jumped up and started to gather my things, but Benzino was persistent. He pleaded with me, saying all he wanted was just to lie there next to me and maybe hold me, promising that nothing would happen. We did that, but after a few minutes, he started to feel me up. I'd had enough, so I got up, grabbed my belongings, and took a cab. On my way to the airport, I had to swallow the fact that even though I'd tried to follow my own professional rule of no fraternizing with my customers, I had absolutely no control over them or their behavior whatsoever.

Was It Because I Swallowed

CHAPTER 17

Artists who were rocking braids weren't the only people I'd approach in the music industry. I stepped to the people behind the scenes as well, like producers and record-label executives.

During Super Bowl XXXVI in New Orleans, my homeboy AG hosted a party at the Sheraton Hotel on Canal Street. Everyone from coast to coast was there, from Mariah Carey to Suge Knight.

When I saw Marion "Suge" Knight, who was once CEO of Death Row Records, my Cali instincts kicked in, and I had to holler at him.

I didn't hesitate to let him know that I was an Atlanta braider who claimed Inglewood, California, as my old stomping ground. I also told him that I'd be visiting Los Angeles soon for the BET Awards and would like the opportunity to braid any artists he was producing so he could see my skills. He and I exchanged numbers, and I called him within days of landing in Los Angeles a month or so later.

Suge said it was cool to hear from me and that we could meet up at his current headquarters, The Row Records, located on Wilshire and San Vincente.

I pulled up to The Row's building, and once upstairs was directed to a main conference room by a cute, biracial girl who appeared to be in her late teens or early twenties.

As I walked down the long corridor, I counted at least five offices. I couldn't help but wonder if Tupac had ever been there. I wondered what kind of relationship he and Suge really had. I couldn't wait to ask Suge all about

Tupac, but I knew there was going to be a time and place for that.

Although I know I told Suge I'd graduated from Georgia State, I wasn't sure that I wanted to tell him I had a criminal justice degree, for fear he might shut me down, thinking I was five-o or some kind of cop wannabe. So if it ever came up, I thought I would switch subjects and tell him about the time I was married to a California inmate and how I visited almost every Los Angeles County jail, from the old to the new county, from Chino to Tehachapi, and finally Corcoran. Hopefully that would throw any po-po theories Suge may have had about me out the window.

I decided not to think about Tupac for the moment and focused on the artist Suge had for me to braid instead. Several minutes later, a young light-skinned rapper came in and sat down, telling me he was Suge's artist.

His hair was wavy, long, and already clean, so all I needed to do was braid it. When I finished, Suge was coming up the elevator. He walked into the conference room, greeted me with a huge hug, and told me that I'd done a great job on his artist's head. He asked if I'd like to go and eat with him and some friends.

"Sure. I never turn down meals," I said.

As he and a few other folks climbed into the SUV, I followed in my compact Chevy rental to Gladstone's Seafood Restaurant in Redondo Beach, twenty-five minutes away.

There were eight of us—including a couple of hired security guys—walking toward the restaurant when Suge pointed out that this same spot happened to be Tupac's favorite seafood restaurant. I was about to follow up with a question about Tupac, but I was beat to the punch by a young man I later learned was trying to intern for The Row.

Suge turned to the guy and said, "Do not ask any questions about Tupac, and I mean any of you!"

After that, I considered not even joining them for dinner. All I really wanted was the 411 on Tupac. It was OK for Suge to talk about Tupac, but no one else could. When anyone did, Suge's demeanor could possibly change from Dr. Jekyll to Mr. Hyde. "Not good," I thought to myself.

As I sat at this huge table with Suge's hired hands and interns, we chose our words carefully, like kids not wanting to upset Daddy. Suge was intimidating, but I didn't let that stop me from enjoying my meal. I still ate like a champ, and the seafood was delicious. After dinner I went my way.

The following day I realized that I'd forgotten to ask Suge to pay me for my braids. We hadn't made any arrangements—like he'd take me out to dinner in exchange for my service—so I called him. I told him I'd like to stop by to get my cheddar because I would be in his neck of the woods eating at my favorite Mexican Restaurant, El Coyote. Suge said it wasn't a problem. He even asked to join me for lunch.

El Coyote has the best authentic Mexican food on earth, hands down as far as I'm concerned. The female servers wear the long, flared, ruffled dresses with colorful prints while the men rock polyester suits with matching sombreros. It's awesome.

As I approached the gate of The Row this time, Suge told me to park my vehicle and to jump in an all black van with him and his security guards. Once at the restaurant, Suge and I sat outside and finally got to have a one-on-one conversation. But when I looked into his dark eyes, they seemed hollow, almost as if he was empty on the inside. I didn't bother to ask about my hero, Tupac, because I was afraid that his face would turn to stone the way it had at Gladstone's the day before.

The bottom line was that I was scared of him. When we left the restaurant and they took me back to my rental, I couldn't get away from him fast enough. I jumped in my car and rolled down my window because I still needed to be paid. Suge handed me a hundred dollars and had the damn nerve to kiss me on my lips. I couldn't do anything except swallow the shock I was in.

He jacked me for a kiss, and there wasn't shit I could do about it. I have asked myself over and over what I did to make him think he could kiss me on my lips. I wasn't fucking feeling him like that at all and sure as hell hadn't given him any reason to make him feel I was. But I was too scared to boss up and ask him what the hell he was doing. Instead, I drove off in my rental, thankful to have gotten what I did out of him. Two meals, a hundred dollars, and I was still breathing.

Suge wasn't the only record-label executive that I'd stepped to. Back in Atlanta, Big Meech of BMF and J Rock of Sin City Mafia had also allowed me to be the regular braider of their artists, Bleu DaVinci, Ooowee, and Dep Wuds. I was getting to service all sorts of folks, doing something I enjoyed anyway and I loved it.

CHAPTER 18

One of the many perks of braiding pro athletes was that I got to attend their games. Once when I was at a Hawks game in the clubhouse section of Phillips Arena, I saw a guy surrounded by an entourage of people. They all stood around ogling and catering to him like he was an Egyptian Pharaoh. It was the rookie Michael Vick.

About a year later, I saw him standing in front of the nightclub Vision on Peachtree Street. I couldn't help but notice him because my homegirl Kortni was totally bugging out, thinking that Mike Vick was looking in her direction, trying to get her attention. I laughed because he wasn't even thinking in her direction. I was like, "Girl, if you don't chill out..."

Both times I spotted Mike Vick, he looked unapproachable. I didn't want to walk up on him, kissing up like most groupies and sports fans. He didn't have any braids, so there wasn't too much he could do for me.

However, a couple of years later, he had grown his hair out and was rocking braids. His then teammate Warrick Dunn referred me to him as a local braider.

Warrick was an angel as far as I'm concerned. He dialed Mike's number right in front of me, and I was able to get an appointment on the spot for the very next day. So of course the next time I saw Warrick in Tonsorials Edge Barbershop on Edgewood in Atlanta, I had to thank him like crazy for looking out for a sista.

Mike lived just thirty miles or so north of Atlanta, at the Country Club at Sugarloaf. When I pulled up to his subdivision, I had to be let in by security. This happened to be the same subdivision Mack 10 lived in with his then wife, T-Boz.

Mike's home was three stories tall, off-white, and sat at the end of a cul-de-sac. His front door had Greek-looking columns supporting the covered carport. Inside, the floor in the atrium was entirely marble, with a distinguished black-and-white pattern directly in the center of the foyer. Straight ahead was a vaulted cathedral ceiling over a sunken living room. It reminded me a bit of Michelangelo's Sistine Chapel ceiling in Vatican City, except this room had large bay windows exposing a stunning view of what appeared to be a small man-made lake. It was such a lovely home, quite impressive for any man to own, especially someone just twenty-four.

After formally introducing myself, I thought, "Yummy, he's a cutie," but he looked just a little too small to play pro football. I thought Mike had to have a lot of heart to be his size and play against so many men that seemed twice as big.

As we walked farther into his kitchen, I explained my services and decided we could get started by washing his head in the double kitchen sink.

Mike's hair felt just like Mikki Moore's. His hair badly needed straightening with a hot comb, but Mike said he didn't like that idea because he was used to the fat, natural rough-looking braids.

Mike didn't understand that pressing his hair would make it look much neater, last longer, and produce better results with any style. So after I washed and blow-dried his hair, I convinced him to let me press it for the first time ever. Mike stiffened up during that process and only relaxed when I was no longer holding the hot comb.

Just as he began to open up and talk to me, his cousins and brother came into the kitchen, out of nowhere.

Mike introduced me to everyone, but I didn't care to talk to any of them. I had the king in my hands already. I just wanted to remain one-on-one with Mike, the way I had been up until then. But for some reason his younger brother, cousin and friends wouldn't leave us alone and began talking loud, playing music, and play fighting with one another. A few of them even had the nerve to try to shoot game at me.

After a while Mike lost his patience and finally said, "Let the lady alone so she can do my hair!" They all left and went downstairs to the basement, and I was able to finish his hair.

Although Mike allowed me to press his hair, I could tell he wasn't happy with the results because my braids looked half the size of the ones he'd previously had and said he preferred.

The next appointment with Mike, I had my cousin LaShawn come with me because she was cuter and younger than me. I figured I could use her to distract his family and friends. Instead, Mike inquired about her.

This time around I followed my usual process without finding out whether Mike wanted his hair pressed or not. I think he was against my pressing his hair, but he didn't say anything. He ended up letting me do what I wanted. After I was done, I told him that his braids wouldn't look professionally done without the pressing. Still, he never called me back for another appointment. I can only assume that since I was so persistent about pressing him, I lost him as a client.

I had no choice but so swallow the fact that doing what I wanted as a stylist cost me Mike Vick's VIP clientele. It was a very valuable lesson, and trust me—I've learned to give people what they ask for regardless of what I think they should have done to their hair.

Was It Because I Swallowed

CHAPTER 19

As luck would have it, R&B artist Terrence Quaites, aka TQ, formerly of Cash Money Records, invited me to New Delhi, India. My business couldn't get any sweeter than that.

TQ was in India filming the movie *Rockin' Meera*, a Bollywood film. Bollywood was India's version of Hollywood. I couldn't believe I'd finally made it to an actual movie set after all the years of living in Los Angeles.

I felt blessed because my braids had already hit CD covers, magazines, videos, and pro-sports venues. Now they would be on a movie set *in another country*. Visiting another continent just to provide a service was a great accomplishment. Working in corporate America couldn't have landed me here, not unless I'd made it to CEO status. This was a dream come true, not to mention it sure beat braiding at any Atlanta recording studio. Not that I was dissing my regular gigs; this was just better.

When TQ called and invited me, I played it off nonchalantly, but I was overjoyed. He said all I would need to do was get a couple of shots, one for typhoid and one for malaria. Almost every country has a series of shots that are recommended to tourists before they enter.

After a nearly fifteen-hour flight, I finally exited the plane in New Delhi. The air smelled vaguely familiar and immediately brought back childhood memories of visiting the circus for the first time. I knew I couldn't speak or read the language, so I followed everyone else off the plane, figuring they were heading to baggage claim, where I wanted to go.

Once I'd retrieved my luggage, I left the airport. Dozens of loved ones were outside awaiting passengers. It was already dark outside, but not too dark for me to see a sign with my name on it. That was such a relief because TQ and I hadn't discussed exactly who'd be picking me up.

The man resembled the typical Indian man; he was five foot eight with silky jet-black hair and tangerine-colored skin. It was obvious he spoke very little English because he could only tell me his name and ask me mine. As long as he took me to where I needed to be, we were good.

He grabbed my bags, and I followed him to his early 2000s compact Toyota. While walking through a nearly empty parking lot, we passed several small animals running freely about, and I just tripped. I assumed they were puppies at first, but they looked more like little hyenas with golden-brownish spots everywhere. I was grateful they weren't in a pack. They really looked hungry and appeared to be searching for food. It made my heart sink.

As we drove off, I didn't understand why those puppies didn't have any owners. But as we drove into the heavily populated areas of the city, I saw sheep, cattle, and other livestock roaming just as free.

This trip was nothing like my previous trips to Greece, Italy, or London. I felt like I was on another planet. There were people traveling on scooters and rickshaws, three-wheeled bikes that pulled passenger carts behind them.

After the first few hours of our 650-mile trip to Gajsner, I asked if we could pull over at a gas station so I could use the restroom.

The bathroom had no front door and no doors on the stalls. Each stall looked like a big shower with a drain on the floor. When I looked up, I saw hundreds of lizards on the walls and ceiling. I ran screaming for my life, waving my hand at my throat, gesturing in a slicing motion that I wasn't going to be using the bathroom in there. I'm sure the driver understood what I was saying because he laughed out loud.

There was no way I was going to use that restroom. I held it in.

We hopped back in the vehicle and drove until the sun began to rise. Once the sun was up, I saw nothing but endless red sand, elephants and camels, and even natives squatting to use the restroom in the open fields.

Once we did stop to use the restroom and I returned to the car it was surrounded by a handful of cows. They seemed harmless. They just looked hungry as if they were starving so I began feeding them some of the saltine crackers I was snacking on. Those couple of cows turned into a dozen quick. Finally, the driver had to intervene because by then the entire box was empty and more cows were heading in my direction.

Everything was different, from the soil to the people to the sun's rays. It had to have been a hundred degrees out there. Thankfully, we were in an air-conditioned vehicle.

Once we reached the entrance of the fortresslike structure called Gajsner Palace, I couldn't believe my eyes. I later learned that this palace had once been under British rule but was now used as a four-star hotel with very few renovations at all. I couldn't believe that my decision to step out on faith had landed me here—in a real palace on a different continent. Man, God is great!

Was It Because I Swallowed

CHAPTER 20

Throughout the years and regardless of my profession me and my homegirls did whatever was necessary to attend all the big events, like the Super Bowl, NBA All-Star games, Essence Festivals, BET Awards, and pro-boxing events, just to name a few. We even considered attending the Kentucky Derby just to see if we could come up on high rollers there. We were on a mission to find all the ballers so we could get in their pockets and bask in their fame.

When I look back, I can't believe I was posted up at those types of events, looking like a million dollars with my painted-on minidresses and expensive purses and shoes. I thought that if I got attention from men with money, they'd always take care of me, and I would never have anything to worry about. All along I didn't have a pot to piss in or a window to throw it out of.

One Memorial Day weekend, my neighbor, Candice, invited me to join her and some friends on a trip from Atlanta to Miami. Candice said a friend of hers was a chauffer for a limo service and had been hired out to drive there. It was a free trip, so how could I have turned it down?

I knew JoJo would be there anyway. He even offered to fly me in, but I told him that I'd be riding with friends. But I also told him I'd definitely do his hair while I was there if he wanted me to. Money was still money.

Candice was a tall, thin, light-skinned, pretty model chick originally from Miami. She was also a member of ex-rapper Mase's Sane Ministries at the time. Her cousin Gia, who also joined us, was just as cute—not as tall, but way more curvaceous than Candice. Gia was the little girl who appeared in a music video for the once popular kid R&B group Another Bad Creation.

It was Thursday around midnight when our driver pulled up to our apartments in Buckhead and introduced himself. He told Gia, Candice, and me to enjoy the ride as we loaded the limo's trunk with our precious belongings. He was a young black brother with great energy who made the ten-and-a-half-hour drive much smoother than I'd expected. I knew from having driven to Miami once before from Atlanta that it could be insanely boring. Gia, Candice, I, and another gentleman all played cards, talked, and slept off and on for the majority of the drive.

It was just after eleven when we arrived in Miami the next morning, eager to check into our room at the Marriot on Collins Avenue. Candice, Gia, and I split the room three ways, making each of us responsible for one night at $109. It felt nothing like the time I'd split a room three ways in Las Vegas with those chicks. Instead, I had a feeling this would be just as memorable minus the haters.

As soon as we got to our room, I dropped my luggage, took a shower, and got dressed in cool cotton clothes because it was already a hot day. By noon I was headed down Collins Avenue, hauling my products in hand for seven blocks until I reached JoJo's leased condo on Fifteenth. Along the way I ran into the rapper Fabolous, who happened to be walking with his crew. I handed him my card, chatted with him for a moment, and continued on to my destination.

Fabolous, who was wearing braids himself at the time, told me that he didn't need his hair done that weekend but that he'd be in the Atlanta area soon and would surely give me a call.

As in the past, I approached JoJo's concierge and asked to be let up to his condo. After braiding JoJo, I headed back to my room to meet up with my Playboy bunny–looking friends for an afternoon of frozen drinks with umbrellas. As we indulged in margaritas at Wet Willy's, we started to talk about our options for that evening. Just then I got a call from JoJo, asking if we'd like to join him for dinner and an evening of partying.

I ran it by Candice and Gia, and they agreed it would be all good. We headed back to our room to get dolled up for a night of fun.

I decided to wear a retro Bill Hallman orange, chocolate brown, and beige minidress with the belly cut out in a square shape, exposing my belly button. With that I would wear some fierce shoes I'd purchased in London years earlier. I didn't think my roommates were ready for what I had on, but they still looked cute.

We met JoJo on the bottom level of his condo, where there was a patio restaurant. The hostess seated us at outside tables. We all ate different entrées of seafood and steak and had all the drinks we could swallow.

Once we were all nice and full, JoJo summoned his driver to pull around and pick us up.

The six of us headed to a club where there was standing room only. It was so packed, we couldn't all stay together. Luckily, I could see JoJo from any part of the club because he was so tall. After being pushed and shoved around for most of the night, my girls and I figured it was time to go.

When I informed JoJo, he told me that I hadn't been released yet, but that if I did have to leave, to make sure I answered his call later on that evening. It felt good to know that even though JoJo was surrounded by hundreds of beautiful women, he still wanted to be able to get ahold of me.

Gia, Candice, and I left the club, walked a few blocks, and hailed a cab back to our room. I thought it was a wrap for the night, but at four in the morning, JoJo called and told me to come back to his spot, pronto. Even though I had been paid to braid him earlier, my services apparently hadn't ended. I did as I was told and walked back to his condo so I could put him to sleep just like a baby with a bottle, except he was the bottle, and I did all the sucking.

The next day the girls and I ate brunch on Ocean Drive, then sat out in the hot sun on the beach for a couple of hours. It couldn't have been any better. During the walk back to our hotel, I separated from the girls because I wanted to hustle up a braid customer or two.

I'm a go-getter, and making money never stops for me, so I managed to find some random guy whose braids looked bad enough for me to approach him. His hotel room was next door to the Loews Hotel and not far from me at all. I told him I needed a minute to run and get my products, but I'd be right back.

As I walked back to get my hair products, an older man followed me, saying that his nephew, Kai, wanted to holler at me.

"Yeah, right," I told him.

I started walking faster because the old guy looked a little suspect, and I was wearing a Presidential Rolex, diamond hoop earrings, and a matching ring. This could've been a setup, for all I knew. Then again, I was looking cute in my white terrycloth sweatpants with the matching hat and a Derek Jeter #2 New York Yankee tank top. Maybe his infamous nephew really was down the street, wanting to holler. It wasn't like I hadn't gotten with a big-time NBA player before.

So I turned around and told the old man to lead the way. I was kind of curious to see if this dude was for real.

While walking back, all I could think about was how large Kai's name was in the NBA and how many more doors would open up for me in the industry if I became his braider. Shit, I could live large. I couldn't help but get excited, and I started really hoping this man wasn't off his meds and hadn't just broken out of the psych hospital.

I continued walking, and the closer I got, the more I could see that the man we were walking toward was in fact Kai. He was sitting on a motor scooter under a shaded palm tree. I wanted to melt into the sidewalk with each step I took closer to him, but I played it cool.

When I approached him, he asked me what my name was and if I had a minute to talk.

"Celeste, and I sure do," I replied. I couldn't believe that I was standing in front of Kai, with his fine, braid-wearing, rough, neck-tatted-up ass. His cushiony-looking lips and tangerine-and-caramel skin made me want to scratch and sniff him just like the perfume ads in magazines, except I wanted to do nasty things to him, too.

I gave him my card and told him I was a braider from Atlanta and would love to have the opportunity to braid his hair. At this point I wasn't sure if he and JoJo were friends, so I wanted to keep it professional. Kai told me it was good to know that I braided and that he would call me later. After that, I skipped back to the hotel to share the news about my potential new client.

The next day Candice, Gia and I were eating brunch on the beach when I got a call from Kai. He didn't want his hair braided; instead, he wanted to meet up with me later on a personal tip, just to hang out. I was cool with that, too.

While the girls and I were sunbathing that afternoon, Candice said that she and Gia were planning to meet up with a couple of friends of hers and were making reservations for all of us to have dinner later at a five-star seafood restaurant.

After dinner, we all decided to hit up Club Oasis. It was only around eleven, but the line to get in the club was crazy long. The bouncer said that unless we purchased a table at $500, we weren't getting in. As we all stood outside the club behind the metal security railings, we decided we'd all pitch in and pay $100 each.

Just as we were about to huddle to gather our money, Joc, a NFL defensive end, walked up to the bouncer, who quickly moved the barrier for him. I stepped away from my girls and shouted to Joc just as he was about to enter the front door of the club. He turned around and smiled, happy to see me because we hadn't seen each other in a few months. He and I had kicked it intimately off and on for years, but it wasn't anything serious.

As he walked toward us, I noticed that Candice and Gia now looked dumbfounded because Joc was 230 pounds of pure chocolate. He was a stallion of a man if I'd ever seen one.

Candice whispered, "Celeste, who is that god?" Gia just looked like she was stuck on stupid.

As I introduced Joc to everyone, I asked him if he would mind if we all came in with him. He said that he didn't mind, as long as I hooked up with him later that evening. I joyfully agreed. Joc then turned to the bouncer and had a few words with him. Without even exchanging any money, we all were let in.

I was relieved and felt quite like the hero that night in my crew. The club was one of those outside/inside deals, so we were all over the place. For some reason, it didn't get as packed as we'd expected, and by one o'clock we were all ready to bounce.

Just as we were leaving, Kai called and asked if he could pick me up to hang out. Hell yeah! I told the girls not to wait up, and I was out of there.

As I joyfully skipped around the corner from the club, where I told Kai I'd be, he pulled up, and I jumped into a black SUV with him, his driver, and another guy. I noticed that we were being tailed by a similar SUV and assumed that those following us were either security or his entourage.

That evening I was rocking an all-pink United Colors of Benetton outfit. It was a knitted top and matching capri pants with a white leather handbag and matching wedge shoes. I definitely stood out because Kai and his entire crew all seemed to be dressed in black.

Both SUVs pulled out into traffic and drove for a few miles. We were stopped at a red light when a man who looked like the uncle that had stopped me the day before dodged in front of our truck and ran across the street, crossing several lanes of traffic.

Kai's driver said, "There goes your crazy uncle again."

The man was now yelling as he ran toward the Rolexx strip club.

Kai laughed and said we all needed to go in there after him because he wasn't leaving his family like that.

We entered the club and followed behind Kai, who was now being referred to by another name. We walked up some stairs and were seated at two separate small, black round-top tables. Kai ordered two bottles of Dom Perignon at $500 a pop, the way one would order bottled water. He didn't even flinch when the waitress asked for the $1,000.

The club reminded me of a small opera. Its auditorium balcony seats were up so high that we could barely see the strippers onstage below. We had only been there for thirty minutes when Kai abruptly stood and signaled that we needed to leave.

All of us piled back into the SUVs and drove toward his hotel room at the Delano on Collins Avenue. When we pulled up front, Kai and I stayed seated in the back of the truck until Swizz Beats, whose real name is Kasseem Daoud Dean, a New York City music producer, walked up to the back window and began talking to Kai. I wanted to say more to Swizz than just hello—like thank you for the Ruff Ryders and DMX's *Blood of my Blood* CD— but didn't because I didn't want to seem like a groupie.

I said absolutely nothing and played quiet, like I was in time-out, while they talked to each other. The thing was, I didn't want to do anything to make Kai change his mind about choosing me to be his flavor for the night. I know it was wrong of me to even be there. I knew he was married, but that night I didn't care. I'd had more than enough time to walk away, but I didn't.

A few minutes later, out of nowhere gunshots rang out. Kai, Swizz, and I were forced to retreat into the Delano lobby for cover. Apparently some guys did a drive-by shooting at some folks who were just walking along the sidewalk.

During all the commotion and chaos, Joc called. I looked over at Kai and thought, "I'm not going anywhere." I only felt bad momentarily about not answering because I thought this might be my only chance to get with Kai, so I let my phone continue to vibrate in my purse and stayed with my new boy toy for the night.

When we got up to Kai's room, he definitely made me sure the decision I had made was the right one.

He walked me to his bed, and we both sat down. I couldn't stop looking at him. He was so fine that my hormones started to go berserk. I felt goose bumps popping up all over my skin. I wanted him so much that I wanted to get right to it. Fuck foreplay.

I stood up and bent over to kiss his lips. Then I worked my way around his neck and upper torso as he grabbed my ass cheeks. His dick started to grow big and thick, satisfying my need to know that his love below matched his bad-boy attitude.

I couldn't help myself. I had to hold his soldier in my hand because it looked savory through his pants. I quickly unzipped his pants and took it out. It was just as beautiful as he was, and I couldn't wait to ram it into my cave. I wasn't ready to taste him just yet, so I pulled down my pants as he dropped his.

As I lay on the bed, he strapped up and got on top of me. I couldn't help but look into his sexy brown eyes as he tried to fit his dick inside my inner walls. At first it was hard getting it in because his shit was plump, but when it was finally in, we fucked for at least twenty minutes straight. Not that I was counting, but I did love every second of it.

To this day, that night is still memorable to me. I definitely believed Kai was worth standing Joc up for. That is, until the next day when I called Kai during the limo ride back to Atlanta, only to have one of his boys answer, laugh, and hang up in my face. I couldn't help but feel microscopic, like a piece of lint on the limo's carpet, for ten hours straight.

Was It Because I Swallowed

CHAPTER 21

I felt used, insulted, and pissed all at once. I knew I'd left myself open to be treated like a one-night stand, but I expected Kai to at least be more tactful. It was a little too late, but I regretted standing Joc up for Kai. During the drive back to Atlanta, I was overloaded with emotions and had no choice but to swallow the disrespect that had just taken place. Candice could tell something was bothering me because she kept asking me if I was OK. I said yes, but in reality I wasn't. I started to tear up but played it off. I had gone as low as any woman could have and had sex with two men during the same weekend.

I had to persuade myself I was worth more than how I was feeling at that moment. If I was the low-down skank I was feeling like, Joc, Kai, and JoJo wouldn't have chosen me to entertain them in Miami that Memorial Day weekend. There were hundreds of other gorgeous, model-looking chicks ripe for the picking, but I ended up with not one, but three millionaires choosing me.

However, I didn't feel validated the way I had in the past. Instead, I felt like I had just been taken by Kai and that I got exactly what I had coming to me because I *knew* he was married and should've been off-limits.

And even though I was still JoJo's braider, I was looking like the loser in that equation, too. Just thinking about it hurt me because, once again, I had accomplished absolutely nothing by fucking yet another NBA player. Just the same stupid mistake replayed and replayed. I should have had enough of double backing on my word, fucking them, and walking away with nothing. Hell, my bank account was still in the negative.

I needed to create preventive measures so that another mishap like that one wouldn't happen again. As bad luck would have it, I became stranded during the 2003 NYC blackout with JoJo and the whole USA Men's Basketball team at the Ritz Carlton for the entire weekend.

Despite the potential severity of the situation, in my mind I still compared it to being in Wonderland, and I was Alice. I would be stuck, at least for the time being, with fine young black millionaires. I was determined to avoid another penis overload like Memorial Day weekend in Miami.

This would be my second year accompanying JoJo to the USA Men's Basketball game. The roster this time included Tracie McGrady, Vince Carter, Mike Bibby, and Tim Duncan, just to name a few.

New York City was always such a beautiful place to visit. I loved the Broadway shows, the shopping, the magnificent restaurants, and the excitement and energy it offered. And it was my deceased brother's favorite city, so I seemed to connect with him whenever I was there.

I arrived at the Ritz Carlton in Central Park early Thursday afternoon, just after flying in from Atlanta. I immediately got busy on JoJo's hair because I wanted to shop for the rest of the day.

A couple of hours later, Chris Aire, JoJo's jeweler, came into his hotel suite. He walked into the room, introduced himself to me, and opened up his briefcase on top of the coffee table. Inside were several small velvet bags containing different types of diamonds. He had everything from necklaces to rings and watches for JoJo to see. Chris was a charming Nigerian who seemed highly educated yet very Americanized. He hardly had an African accent at all. Chris said that he was the jeweler to the stars in Los Angeles and even compared himself to Jacob the Jeweler out of New York City.

A few minutes later, Tracy McGrady walked into the room and asked us if our power was off. I had never met Tracy, but I did know that he was considered a top-ten player in the NBA.

JoJo, Chris, and I had no idea what he was talking about. Tracy walked over by the window and looked out, and we all walked over to see what the big deal was. Looking down from JoJo's seventh-floor window to the streets below, we could see the streets filling with people. The traffic was backing up for what looked like miles.

Cars and buses stopped and honked their horns as people multiplied in the streets. All the people seemed to be looking up toward the sky for answers. The subways entrances started to congest. People were coming up from them, looking just as bewildered as those contemplating going down. No one seemed to know exactly what was happening, and all the vehicles were now at a standstill. It was crazy.

Up in the room, we all assumed that if there was a power problem, it would only be a matter of time before the issue was corrected.

After almost forty-five minutes of waiting, JoJo instructed me to go downstairs to the front desk and check in, just in case I became stranded and the power didn't come back on. I was due to fly back to Atlanta that evening, but from the looks of things, that wasn't going to happen. I was grateful to get a room the moment I did because the Ritz was already almost at capacity.

While I was securing my room at the front desk, the lobby began to fill up with people walking in from off the streets, going to the bar, and checking the availability of rooms.

With my room key in hand, I walked over and asked the concierge how dismal the situation was. The friendly-looking middle-aged black man said that it wouldn't be too bad because the hotel was being run on generators and was still operational with the exception of the kitchen, which was now closed. It was obvious there was nothing I could do but go to the bar and order a Belvedere apple martini—my favorite alcoholic drink. I had a feeling it was going to be a long night.

While I was at the bar, Chris, the jeweler, came back downstairs and tapped me on my shoulder. To my surprise, he was now trying to play matchmaker. He said that he had someone who wanted to meet me. As I asked him who, I took a sip of my martini and looked up to see Chris gesturing toward the man standing a few feet behind him. It was Kai. I almost choked on my martini.

I really wanted to slap the caramel color off Kai's face. Instead, I wiped my mouth, stood up, and slowly walked over to him with Chris, but I couldn't stop thinking to myself, "This motherfucker fucked me last year in Miami and didn't even remember me, and now he wants to be reintroduced?"

I couldn't believe he was standing inches away from me again and had the audacity to ask me what my name was as I approached him. I had something in store for his ass. I went right along and pretended that we had never met. I gave him my cell phone number and room number and told him it was a pleasure meeting him, with every intention of fucking with his head.

I walked back to my seat at the bar. Chris finished talking to Kai and eventually joined me again. As Chris and I continued our conversation, he said that he was waiting for another appointment with some *Robb Report* magazine executive. I could barely process what Chris was saying because I was still in shock about what had just happened. I had been so perplexed about what had happened last year. Now Kai was making it worse by trying to make me feel like a Raggedy Ann doll, like he could just pick me back up and play with me whenever he felt like it. That wasn't right, and Kai needed to be stopped and taught a lesson.

An hour or two had passed. I hadn't realized it, but the martinis were starting to get the best of me. I didn't want to be the girl at the bar that's been there too long, so I got up and took the many flights of steps up to my room to freshen up.

Although the hotel was still operational, it was apparent that the power situation was more serious than we'd assumed. The city had completely shut down. Thousands of people were stranded, but lucky for me I was at the Ritz in an air-conditioned lobby and didn't have to suffer through what many of the New Yorkers were experiencing.

The later it got, the darker it became outside. I decided to venture out to find something to eat. At first I was concerned about my own safety. Blackouts are a perfect opportunity for folks to get robbed or raped.

But since it was only a couple of years after 9/11, the NYC residents seemed united, as if they were looking out for each other. The air felt calm and peaceful for some reason. I couldn't explain it.

Although I had not been an eyewitness to the 9/11 incident, it was the only way I could justify the feeling I had about the unexplained peace in the city that night as I walked down the dark block. As I walked past Mickey Mantel's restaurant, stopping in front of Trump Towers, it seemed much safer that night in New York than the dozens of other times I had been there. There was even an ice-cream truck in front of the hotel. It was an eerie feeling, as if spirits were flying above us, protecting everyone.

When I got back, the hotel lobby was filled with NBA players, including Tracy McGrady and his cousin by marriage, Vic, Kai, and others. As I moved freely back and forth from my room to the lobby, Vic kept trying to get my attention by saying, "Daaammmn," and "Hey, hey, yo."

Whenever I'd walk past him, shaking what my grandmother gave me, he'd say something right in front of Kai, and it felt great.

Just before I went up to my room to call it a night, I started a conversation with a woman who was an art dealer for all of the Ritz Carltons. I asked her how she liked her job. She said it was awesome because she was able to travel all over the world.

Traveling, she met her husband of ten years. He had to have been very successful because this chick was rocking a ten-carat canary-diamond wedding ring. It was amazing, and she told me that she'd earned every stone in it. "Why can't that shit happen to me?" I thought. The ring was so amazing that I walked her over to Tracy, Vic, Kai, and now JoJo and made sure they all got a glimpse of the stone.

To my surprise, the following year JoJo gave a similar stone as an engagement ring to his daughter's mother, Mela. My bubble burst when I found out because I wanted a ring like that one day too.

At midnight the electricity still hadn't come back on, so I decided to call it a night. When I finally got back to my room on the sixteenth floor, it was so hot that I was forced to take a cold shower and sleep practically naked. I felt like I was in the slave quarters and my master, JoJo, was on the lower level. Just after I got into bed, JoJo popped up at my room, checking on me to see if I had someone with me. Seeing that I was alone, he was satisfied and left.

Thirty minutes later, Kai called my room and asked me to come to his room. I said that I would be right down, then immediately took my ass back to sleep. He called again. I apologized for being late and said I was on my way. I hung up and again went back to sleep.

He was persistent. I could just imagine him lying there holding his jimmy because his ass knows he remembered me. I got a good laugh out of that.

He continued to call, but I stopped answering the phone. The following morning when I awoke around ten, the lights were back on in certain sections of the city. We were in Central Park, and I was sure that was why our lights were among the first to come back on.

After I got dressed and went downstairs, I immediately ran into Tracy McGrady, whom I'd forced myself on, as he was about to jump into a chauffeured Mercedes to Brooklyn. Tracy was not bad looking at all, with the exception of that one sleepy wandering eye.

Tracy said he could tell that I was an easygoing person who loved to joke around. "Why not?" I told him. Life is too short, and if laughter makes us live longer, then I will crack jokes until then.

I asked Tracy what was going on in Brooklyn. He said that his little brother was trying to purchase some jerseys and other accessories with his credit card, but the store's owner didn't believe he was Tracy's brother. So

Tracy had to show up in order for his brother to use the card. Personally, I thought the store's owner wanted Tracy to show up so he could take pictures of him to add to his store's celebrity-photo collection.

Tracy's little brother and barber were at the store when we got there, and Tracy handled the situation easily. Tracy's little brother and barber were just as cool as Tracy, and I even got a T-MAC jersey from his barber the following week when I followed the team to Puerto Rico. After Tracy finished up at the store, we headed back to the hotel. When we stepped out of the Mercedes, Fat Joe was out in front of our hotel.

Fat Joe and Tracy apparently knew each other because Fat Joe was saying something about a party that JoJo was hosting at Jay Z's 4040 Club. Even though Fat Joe said he wouldn't be attending, he asked if we were going with JoJo.

When I went up to JoJo's room to ask about the event, he introduced me to the female that was coordinating it. She said she was on her way to go get a weave added into her hair and—hearing I was a braider— asked if I could braid her hair so that the weave could be sown into it. I said sure, and after I finished, I didn't even charge her, like a dummy.

She, in return, gave me a pass to enter JoJo's party that night at the 4040 Club. Not that I needed it because I could've just gone with him, but I thanked her anyway. Come to find out her pass didn't even allow me in VIP. It was OK because Tracy vouched for me to get in the VIP section upstairs.

When I stepped out of the VIP room to freshen up, I saw Kai at the bottom of the steps. He had just entered the club and was already surrounded by at least a half dozen women when he noticed me. He fingered me to come to him, and I thought, "He must be joking." I fingered back for him to come up to me instead.

What would I look like walking down to him while he was surrounded by a gang of women? Immediately he excused himself from his entourage of groupies and climbed the steps toward me. When he and I were face-to-face, he asked me what had happened the night before. I told him I couldn't believe he hadn't called me after we had slept together in Miami less than a year ago, and then to ask to be reintroduced didn't make it better. I told him, for the record, that he was a fantasy fuck. I was happy to have crossed that off my list, and I wouldn't need to see him anymore.

To be honest, I would've loved to fuck the shit out of him again, but I had to stand firm and make him regret disrespecting me by playing me like that.

I thanked him for the wonderful sex I did get, and then I left him standing there, his mouth open, staring at my fine, round ass as I walked away.

After stepping off on Kai, I was excited about getting back to the VIP area to watch Vic play with his featured PlayStation NBA video game.

Vic was one of the NBA players being sponsored by ESPN that evening along with JoJo. While he was playing with the joystick, I had to stop myself from wanting to play with his stick that I hoped would bring me joy.

Vic may have been physically playing the game, but I noticed he was simultaneously talking to me with his eyes. I knew he wanted to get with me from the night before when he kept trying to get my attention. So when he asked me for my cell number before we left the VIP area, I gladly gave it to him.

He called me from the cab on the way back to the hotel. As soon as I returned to the hotel, Vic was at my door. We talked from three in the morning until seven.

Vic must have thought he would talk my draws up off me that night, but it didn't work. He was charming, witty, and clever at getting what he wanted, but because of my NBA-player mishaps, that wasn't going to go down just yet. His energy was awesome, and I was very attracted to him. Even though he wasn't that easy on the eyes, I was impressed with his level of intelligence and great conversation skills.

During our early morning conversation, the way he moved real close to me and talked to me with his face just inches away from my pussy, as if he had his knife and fork with him, let me know it was time for him to leave. When he stood up, I saw that he had an enormous ego in his pants, explaining his sometimes cocky behavior.

I wasn't going to have a penis overload, but it would be difficult with Vic because of how huge the man's penis looked, even through his clothes. Before he left, Vic and I discussed continuing our conversation the following evening.

The next day Vic, JoJo, Kai, Tracie, and some other players left to host a golf benefit as a favor to one of Vic's longtime friends. They were gone all day, and I was beginning to get bored. Fortunately, Michelle was visiting from Richmond that same Saturday with some friends. They visited me at the Ritz around four, and we all headed to the bar.

Of course, thanks to JoJo, the drinks were on my room tab. We took the table nearest the lobby door so we could see who entered or exited. Apparently, my friends didn't believe top-ten NBA players were there until they witnessed it for themselves. For the next couple of hours, we had great conversation and a great time as they shouted the names of players they recognized.

"Mike Bibby!" one of them yelled.

"Tim Duncan!" the other shouted. It was hilarious. Before they left to get ready for their evening, my Puerto Rican girlfriend, Cindy, called.

Cindy later showed up with a couple of Dominican friends, Leslie and Rai, who also got their drink on. We eventually took it up to my room.

While we were partying in my room, Vic called, saying he was approaching my door.

"Time for y'all to leave!" I said. And just as Cindy and her girls were stepping to the door, he knocked. They all said hello to Vic, but as soon as he turned around, Cindy did her giddyup-horsey impression 'cause she knew I was about to ride Vic like a horse.

Finally, a real African American Mandingo was here, I thought to myself. I told Vic that I needed to jump in the shower but that I'd only be a few minutes. As I dried off, I asked Vic if he wouldn't mind lotioning me down. I sort of felt guilty because he was the pro athlete and he should have been the one getting massaged. No way was I going to stop him as he rubbed my shoulders, arms, legs, and butt with lotion, my vaginal lips started to throb, and I knew the moment of truth was at hand.

I know it was only the second day, but it was a start. Vic now had permission to get as close as he wanted and have his own tasting session of me. He was packing so tough that I had to ask him if he had a special jock strap to hold his penis to his thigh because it looked like it could interfere with his game as he ran up and down the court. He laughed out loud and said he didn't.

For the next two days, Vic pleased me in more ways than I'd ever imagined. He must've liked to please women because he was very proactive, often talking me through the intimate process, and I loved every minute of it. At that moment I didn't feel as bad about the hit-and-run that Kai had pulled on me. Then again, after New York Vic never called again, either.

Was It Because I Swallowed

CHAPTER 22

I was back at square one.

I'd just left yet another NBA player's hotel room after having sex with him, only to have my phone calls go unanswered afterward, and it was nobody's fault but my own. It was time for me to take responsibility for my behavior and not point fingers. I had allowed myself to be passed around like the ball they handled on the court, and I felt just as dirty.

I must have had a stupid stamp on my forehead. "Braid professional" or whatever I called myself meant nothing if I still had the mind-set of a whore who obviously didn't value herself. I realized I was kidding myself if I thought these guys didn't talk among themselves about me and my loose ways.

"I'm over this shit," I thought. "It's time to change my ways." I'd created a profession based on being able to get next to all those guys, and it had worked. Too bad I hadn't thought beyond that point. I hadn't realized that in any profession, once you make it to the top, there is nowhere else to go but down.

Not much later the braiding trend and getting league money damn near came to a halt, and car repossession and foreclosure seemed inevitable. I was missing payments on my mercedes, condo and associated homeowner fees. I didn't want to have to sell my beloved possessions but I would soon be needing money to pay for food for my dog, myself and other basic living expenses.

I could still get with ball players, but because I wasn't woman art thou loose anymore, they weren't funding me the way they used to.

After a while, my financial situation was so dismal that I felt as if I were in debtor's prison. I had no clue how I was going to get out until I received a call from my favorite pro athlete. I just knew he could save me.

Even though I had stood Joc up in Miami for Kai, I still believed he genuinely cared about me. Although we had never discussed having a committed relationship, he and I had been seeing each other off and on for over four years now.

Joc invited me to Florida to spend yet another birthday with him, which had now become routine since we had spent the previous three together.

Feeling as bad as I was at the time, this invitation was exactly what I needed to lift my spirits. I would be able to hit him up for money to save my house and car and in the process enjoy his most prized possession, his $7 million beach-front home.

Over the years, I had spent time with him at his homes in Nashville, Tennessee, and Moorestown, New Jersey. But being invited to his birth state of Florida, where his family resided, felt like a real opportunity.

I was also praying that maybe Joc was ready to settle down and had narrowed his harem down to a couple of females, me being among the final few since I've been around him for so long. Besides, I knew my time for being someone's wifey was well overdue, not to mention his genes for procreation were phenomenal.

Since Joc was twenty-eight years old at the time, I figured maybe he had gotten tired of the groupies and gold diggers and was ready to play hubby. It was either that or I was suffering from the Cinderella Syndrome.

In preparation for this trip, I invested my last dollars to look the part of the future Mrs. K. I got my hair highlighted and spent an afternoon getting a manicure, pedicure, and bikini wax. I even went to the mall and purchased a sexy, formfitting dress to wear in case he took me out on the town for my birthday celebration.

My e-ticket was waiting for me at the airport, as usual. And when I arrived in Florida, Joc's limo driver was there to greet me. During the ride I didn't talk to the driver because I was saving all my charm and witty conversation for the man who would soon be mine.

As we exited the expressway, I straightened my hair, touched up my lipgloss, and applied fragrant body lotion, wanting to be as irresistible as possible for my man.

When we pulled up to his spot, I was spellbound. Of all his homes, this was the most remarkable. I felt like a queen about to enter *my* luxurious beach-front castle.

As the driver grabbed my bags and led me into the foyer, I couldn't close my mouth. I was in a state of awe. The crib was insane!

High ceilings, marble floors, an ultramodern high-tech kitchen, and huge windows offering picturesque views of the ocean took my breath away. I stood there soaking it all in, imagining all the things Joc and I would say and do to each other during this special visit. I'd finally found my own Barbie dream house to play in, and Joc was my Ken.

My mind drifted as I began to envision our kids running around, playing. I could see myself baby-proofing the rooms. That was when the driver said, "Adios, and nice to meet you," snapping me back to reality.

For a moment I was disappointed that there were no happy-birthday banners hanging over the doorways, but I shook that off.

This home put the houses in *Architectural Digest* and MTV's *Cribs* to shame. From one of the living rooms, I could see the vanishing waterfall pool and Jacuzzi and, at a distance, a boat dock that housed two Jet Skis. In the ocean's horizon stood a lighthouse topping off what had to be one of the most beautiful seascapes I'd ever seen.

Joc, who was still all muscle and fineness, covered with smooth dark-chocolate skin, appeared from the top of the stairs, flashing his dazzling smile. I couldn't have pictured myself being anywhere else.

I was so into Joc that one time when he called and I was driving, I had to pull over: not only did I have to hear his words; I needed to hear his breath between each syllable when he spoke. During one of our many conversations, he had me unknowingly stripping out of my clothes; by the time our conversation ended, I was somehow naked.

Unless you meet this man, you won't understand what I am saying. The handful of female friends that I have introduced him to also thought he was breathtaking.

He would send for me here and there throughout the years, but I was smart enough to know our relationship wasn't exclusive. I wasn't around on a regular basis; I didn't live where he lived. I knew he had to have groupies chasing him. But so what? I sucked it up. He still wanted to see me, so I must have been doing something right. Whenever he called and invited me to wherever he was, I'd drop everything to accommodate him. I wouldn't care what was going on in my life at the moment; it would have to wait.

Joc was everything I ever wanted in a man: tall, dark, handsome, and rich. How could I have ever stood him up?

I couldn't take my eyes off him as my future king swaggered down the staircase and greeted me warmly with a great big hug and a kiss. His hugs were special because his wingspan was eighty-six inches combined with a 5X glove size, the largest in the NFL. I easily got lost in them and his embrace. Face-to-face I was so excited that I literally almost bowed down to him, like, "Hail Caesar!"

We walked into the kitchen and had the typical get-reacquainted conversation: "Good to see you. How have you been?"

Even though it had been a while, our conversation flowed naturally, as if we had never missed a beat. After we'd talked for a few minutes, he gave me a tour.

I wanted to see the entire house. I really did. But I needed to see Joc first—all of him, especially that buddy attached below his waist. During our phone conversations, I had fun telling him explicit details of what I'd do to him the next time I saw him. I promised him that I was going to swallow him whole. If that included his sperm, so be it. That may sound gross, but I've seen people swallow worse.

I listened to Joc as he guided me in and out of one dramatic room after another. We ended up in the main living area, facing the beach. Our conversation slowed, and I seized the moment. I stared at his crotch, anxious to greet my special buddy. I don't know why, but I wanted to do something to him that I had never done with anyone else, even though he wasn't my husband yet. Something to let him know that I was his, all of me, if he wanted me. I would do that by giving him more pleasure than he could stand. I would force him to produce his seed, and I would swallow every single drop of it. Performing that act, I told myself, would certainly let him know I was serious about us.

I unbuckled his pants, which he seemed to welcome. First I began holding his perfect cock in my hand, gently kissing the tip. Then I worked my fat tongue in circles, finally engulfing his entire penis in my hot mouth. I felt like a beast unleashed. I dropped to my knees and continued to suck his dick like it was the last one on earth. He tasted sweeter than I remembered. Even without double dipping it in Hennessey and Coke, the way I often did, it still tasted delicious. When the big moment came, I didn't flinch.

After I finished, I looked up at him, smile on my face and all. He was silent. He looked down at me as if I was a woman he had never seen before.

Joc's mood totally changed, as if he wasn't expecting what I had just done. He appeared repulsed; he could have been thinking, "You nasty bitch!" He had to have been—why else would he slowly pull up his pants, walk away toward the kitchen, and finally disappear up the stairs? I sat on the edge of the couch in disbelief.

My world crashed.

What had I done so terribly wrong? I did just as I had promised. I was confused, nervous, and a little scared. How could swallowing his sperm have affected our relationship? Wasn't that every man's fantasy? Was there a time frame or protocol for swallowing?

I wanted to run behind him and tell him that I had never done *that* before—it was an isolated incident, only for him. Even though he was known in the NFL as the Freak, on that day he made me feel like one. After the incident, he left the house for a little while. I wanted to talk, but he didn't care to hear anything I had to say. When he returned, he stayed up in his room on the third level, eventually jumping in the shower and preparing himself for bed. I finally joined him in his huge king-size bed. I'd never felt so alone with a human being lying beside me.

When I woke up the next morning, which was my birthday, I decided to use his gourmet kitchen to make a feast of eggs, bacon, pancakes, and freshly squeezed orange juice. I'd cooked plenty of meals for Joc before, from smothered cube steak and collard greens to baked turkey pulled from the bone with mashed potatoes and gravy to chocolate butter pound cakes. I'd even done the food shopping and laundry at his other houses.

However, this house seemed cold and empty as I set breakfast on the table. Joc left without touching any of what I had cooked. He didn't say good-bye or even wish me a happy birthday. I don't know whether he went to practice or to work out. He just left.

I picked over my food, cleaned up the kitchen, then changed into a strapless bikini, and retreated to the pool.

The poolside was magnificent. On the stone patio were lawn chairs and a Jacuzzi. Just beyond that was the pool with a cascading infinity waterfall. Alongside the pool was a pathway leading to the dock. I could smell the ocean. The day was beautiful. The water was so brilliantly blue, and the sky was so clear that I swore I could see Cuba in the distance.

After sitting by the poolside, not bothering to take a dip because I didn't want to mess my hair up, I decided to just make myself a Grey Goose apple martini and roll a blunt. Somewhere in between my second martini and blowing circles in the air, the emotions from all the bullshit I'd had to swallow in life up until that point set in. I started to cry and continued until my eyes were red and swollen. I didn't know how to separate my emotions from the situation.

Other than calling my best friend Tonya in Los Angeles, I basically spent the afternoon drinking martinis, smoking blunts, and crying. One martini turned into two, then three, as if they could help to change my finances. Before I knew it, the sun was beginning to set, and although my mind and body were numb due to my intoxication, they weren't too numb to realize that Joc had left me at home alone all day. Did I mention it was my fucking birthday?

When he finally did return, he was without an explanation, a card, or my Carvel ice-cream cake.

I followed him upstairs. I felt like I had nothing to lose, so I explained my dire financial situation and asked him for $5,000. Without giving it a second of thought, he said, "No."

I tried to persuade him to give me the money by telling him that I would lose my condo and my car without his help. He didn't give a damn. I couldn't believe that I had gone *all in*, giving Joc all I that I had to give of myself. For what? I wish I hadn't swallowed and had saved it for my husband instead. If I were smart, I would have gone all in on myself; my own dreams and aspirations would have been accomplished, and I would've been one badass bitch by then.

Like the night before, he went upstairs, showered, jumped into bed, and eventually went to sleep. Later, I climbed in bed next to him and cried myself to sleep.

The next day, Joc left again, but he did return early that afternoon just in time to see me off. As he led me down the stairs and through the foyer, I felt like a convicted woman walking to her execution.

Once we reached the hired car, he leaned over and kissed me on the lips. After the way he'd treated me over the past two days, this nigga had the audacity to kiss me on the lips! I wanted to grab him by the back of the head and ram his face repeatedly into the hood of that limo, screaming, "You motherfucker! After all the years of me fucking and sucking on you! Motherfucker!"

Before getting in the limo, I told Joc that I had no fucking money and wouldn't be able to get my car out of the airport parking deck. Instead of handing me cash, he told the limo driver to give me sixty dollars when he dropped me off at the airport. I couldn't believe it. I cried so much on the way to the airport, I probably lost a pound of water weight in those twenty-four hours.

On the flight home, I kept hearing Mary J. Blige's "Must Be Out My Mind" in my head. I sang the hook aloud, "Must be out my mind to think that you would marry me," over and over again. I didn't have an iPod, an MP3 player, or a headset. I was just what the other passengers probably perceived as one crazy woman belting out, "Don't wanna play house no more."

Finally the flight attendant approached me and asked if I could please quiet down. I felt like saying, "Bitch, don't you understand what I just went through!"

Rejection. The man whose basket I put all my eggs in, the man I wished to spend the rest of my life with, the man I thought would father my children, the man that— dare I say—I was in love with had just treated me like a money-grubbing trick and wouldn't even help me when I told him how bad my situation was.

Over the years, Joc never asked me if I needed money, but when I was financially strapped, I would ask, and he would come through like a champ.

But this last time, for some reason, he couldn't give a shit about my needs. I often wondered if word got back to him about my other NBA- and NFL-player mishaps, and if so, why would he have sent for me as often as he had if he knew I was being passed around among the other league players?

When the plane landed, I realized I was on the verge of losing my condo, my car, my beloved dog, and the love of my life. But when I called to follow up with Joc that night, he didn't answer. So I left a message asking him, "Was it because I swallowed?" I laughed so hard that I hung up and decided to just write about all the bitter and sweet I'd swallowed instead.

Was It Because I Swallowed

CHAPTER 23

I should have known that I needed someone who was ready to balance his professional schedule with taking time out to be with me—someone who saw the good in me and called me his boo. I wanted someone who laughed at all my jokes and thought the world of me, someone I didn't have to ask to spend time with me, but instead made his schedule to include me. But who was I kidding? I was no longer vibrant and voluptuous and nowhere near a spring chicken anymore, either. However, a decade earlier I had been. I just wished then I had known I was never gonna find a keeper in that circle of men anyway. More important is that I shouldn't have even been looking. Proverbs 18 states, "He that findeth a wife findeth a good thing." I had no business being the hunter instead of the hunted. When God is ready, he will send a man to seek me. He's probably sent me a few great men already; I just missed the signs because I was too busy in the fast lane. I had no patience whatsoever in my twenties and thirties. Not to mention when greatness sat directly in front of me, I couldn't discern that it was even there.

In 1998, while on my way to Milan, Italy, I was seated in first class with a Nigerian man who was on his way back to Africa. He had a dark complexion, a large nose, and a thick accent.

His name was Aliko Dangoté. Aliko said he lived in Atlanta but traveled back and forth to Nigeria for his manufacturing business. I never asked for any more information about him because he didn't look tall enough or fit the profile of most of my acquaintances in the league. Instead, his tailored suit, silk tie, and polished shoes said that he was nothing more than a businessman. But there had to be something there; otherwise I never would have exchanged numbers with him. I figured when he did come back to the States, maybe we'd grab a bite together, but that would be the extent of it.

A week later when I'd returned to the States from Italy, I got a call from Aliko, who was still in Africa. During our conversation, I don't know what made me ask him for money, but for some reason I did. Within the hour, there was a $2,000 wire transfer waiting for me.

Wow! That never happened to me with my pro-athlete acquaintances, not unless we at least had sex first.

The next week, Aliko wired me a couple more stacks. I was like, "Damn! Who has money like that?" I was still totally oblivious.

When Aliko returned to the States, I was anxiously awaiting him so that I could show him my gratitude. Aliko suggested we meet at the Thai Castle in Buckhead for dinner. When we finally met up, it felt awkward.

I thanked him for the cash and asked him what he did for a living, but I didn't believe we had anything in common. I found out he was a banker and owned a sugar manufacturing business—yada yada. I wasn't interested in what he had to say. Not only did he not fit my physical profile, but he wasn't rocking a diamond-bezel Rolex, he wasn't on any all-star team lineup, and he didn't have any shoe company contracts like JoJo and Joc.

After our boring dinner date, he invited me to his place. At first I didn't want to go, until I heard him say his house was just down Pharr Road in Buckhead. I knew that any property in the Buckhead area was prime real estate. So I reluctantly followed him in his fairly new Jaguar to a huge, fire-red brick mansion-style home. It was magnificent with its southern charm, but it still didn't prove to me that he was balling out like my NBA buddies.

Back in 1997 the Internet wasn't as sophisticated as it is today, but if I had done my homework, I would have at least known that Aliko was only a millionaire at the time. I regret not probing enough into who he really was while I was in his presence. I should have at least asked him about his family upbringing, experiences he'd had— something. I showed absolutely no interest in them or him. Instead, I had a shallow, gold-digging mind-set that kept me focused on flashy cars, diamonds, and blowing money fast. With that one-track mind, only these things were important to me.

I lacked the wisdom and insight to ask the right questions to ultimately uncover the fact that Aliko had much more to offer than those pro athletes ever could. I obviously wasn't ready to receive the enormous wealth and blessings that were coming Aliko's way.

Over a decade later, and long after he and I lost contact, I decided to Google his name. Not only had his manufacturing business grown into one of the largest in the world—to include cement, textiles, flour, salt, oil, and gas—but his net worth was quoted in *Forbes* in March 2010 as $18 billion. Why couldn't I have seen more in him at the time than just what he looked like? Sadly, I have to admit that he looks way more handsome now than he ever did. Even when a nice man like Aliko stepped to me respectfully—not just wanting sex but wanting to get to know me—I kicked him to the curb and wasn't ready to receive him or the success that soon followed him.

I had no choice but to swallow the mistake of spending too much time chasing young celebrities and their wealth and basking in their fame when I could have stayed still long enough to receive my own.

Was It Because I Swallowed

CHAPTER 24

I often wished someone had taken the time out to instill in me as a young girl that I had value. Having lived the life that I have, I am here to tell all young girls that they have value. I try not to be upset with my elders who at that time had their own agendas. I also know my parents were just kids themselves when they had me, so I'm not blaming anyone. However, my hope is that those reading this will step up to be more proactive with the little girls in their lives by showing them daily how relevant, smart, and successful they can become.

When I was younger, I blamed my one-night stands on drinking and smoking. As for the occasional prostitution, I always told myself I did it because I liked shopping sprees and could always use the money, but in reality there was no excuse for selling my body. If my value had been ingrained in me as a little girl, I would have known that I couldn't be bought, but because I had a body that men loved, I felt that I could use it whenever I wanted to get whatever I needed from a man. Too bad it came back to haunt me when I least expected it.

It happened when I ran into my homeboy, rapper Jay Wayne Jenkins, aka Young Jeezy, at a club in Atlanta. Young Jeezy and I first met at Club 112 in Buckhead a couple of years before he dropped his first CD, *The Snowman*, in 2004. We hung out a couple of times—eating, drinking, and smoking together. Nothing ever really jumped off.

At that time, I had no idea Jeezy was even in the recording studio. So I was really caught off guard when his CD dropped. I was super happy for him and made sure

I went to see him perform one year at the new Atlanta Live nightclub with rapper TI on Thanksgiving Day.

A couple of months after that concert, I saw Young Jeezy again; this time he was out partying at the South Beach club in Atlanta. He was hanging out with a couple of his homeboys from Macon, Georgia. When I spotted him, I was so excited to see him that I had no idea someone was standing directly behind him. Before I could even congratulate him on his recent success with an embrace, this little five-foot-short nigga came around from behind Jeezy and said to me, "I used to love fucking the shit out of you."

He said it right in front of Jeezy and his whole crew. I froze. What could I do? I was speechless. I was thinking, "Say what, now?" But the words wouldn't come out. All I wanted was for this little nigga to disappear.

Kortni, my homegirl with me at the time, busted out laughing her ass off. This was a moment I wished I could erase, but I couldn't. It was happening.

And it's not even like he made it up. He did, in fact, used to fuck me. However, for the record, he definitely wasn't fucking my brains out. Maybe he thought he had, but sometimes sex for me was nothing but theatrics for monetary gain. Believe me, my lips never touched his penis. He only got a chance to fuck because he was an ex–drug dealer back in 1996 and had a major bankroll. I couldn't even remember this fool's name, which was a testament to his not being good in bed. Trust! I had no choice but to swallow the embarrassment of that awkward moment.

Right then, I knew I didn't want something like this to happen to anyone else out there, especially my little cousins and nieces. I can't believe that once upon a time I thought material possessions and money just fell in my lap without any price to pay. In fairy-tale land, they might. But in the real world, nothing is free, and the acceptance of nice new clothes, fine jewelry, and the latest electronics is nothing but a setup. There are absolutely no material possessions worth the price of one's soul.

Was It Because I Swallowed

CHAPTER 25

Over the years, between my big booty (long before butts were popular) and braid hustle, I stayed up close and personal with many celebrities and continued to be in the right place at the right time.

It was great because all I ever wanted was to be surrounded by fine, young black men with plenty of money, fast cars, and expensive things. Too bad none of them had ever told me he wanted me to be the number one girl in his life and that I didn't have to braid for a living or gold-dig anymore. That never happened.

It wasn't until I'd hit rock bottom and reached a stage of self-awareness that I could see clearly, as if the cloud that followed me had suddenly disappeared. I realized that I was so busy trying to be validated by these guys and their material possessions that I couldn't see the fortune within myself. I had obviously missed something, so I starting searching within myself for the answers. I realized that if I needed to see change, I had to become it.

During this rude awakening, I was introduced to Juanita Bynum's *No More Sheets*. The evangelist's book helped me to realize that every man I'd had sex with was now considered a sheet I'd been bound with. And because I'd slept with so many men, I couldn't go backward; instead I needed work at unwrapping each layer individually to cleanse myself of their spirits once and for all. First, I had to accept my loose behavior. With that acceptance, I immediately began to heal. Secondly, I had to read scriptures and inspirational material, pray daily, and abstain from sex altogether. In the meantime, my spirit began to be replenished with the help of occasional fasting and body detoxing. If you do all of this yourself, rest assured you will find yourself and the validation will be yours. I even felt different, almost virtuous, as if the little girl in me had come back. However, I knew nothing about being virtuous, and knew it was time to learn. Juanita's book helped me to purge most of the men that I'd wasted my soul on during those erotic encounters.

My story is real and had to be told. Believe me, I wouldn't have written a book about swallowing if my story's climax wasn't worth it to me. You've got to admit, it was crazy. Even though it turned out that Joc didn't want me, I still thought he was the right one to swallow because I thought I loved him. If he left me for trying to show him, for trying to prove that to him, then so be it. I can't live the rest of my days wondering if he would have stayed if I had done this or hadn't done that. After this last celebrity encounter with Joc, I accepted the consequences and swallowed the fact that because of this infamy, I may never become someone's wife.

Now that everything has been said and done, I can admit that I've made way too many mistakes. I knew I would have to stumble and fall just like everyone else. However, my story is too compelling to not be shared in hopes of helping other young girls. Now that I'm in my prime, I know I can't go back. But for those young lost souls, I hope this helps.

There are two rules I learned from Bill Gates's eleven rules to life that I live by now. His first rule is that life isn't fair, so get used to it. His second rule is that the world doesn't care about your self-esteem; the world expects you to accomplish something before you feel good about yourself.

I now wish I had paid more attention to those regular guys who had plenty of potential. Who knows—in the long run, one of them could have been good for me. Instead I ended up chasing after the right-here, right-now types of men. But those guys who had money to burn were only going to be as faithful as their options anyway. I don't know why I thought I could wait for some pro athlete or celebrity to eventually come around and court me. I was better than that. If I hadn't spent so much time trying to hunt for a man solely based on whether he could give me that lifestyle of the rich and famous I thought I wanted, I would've been able to stay still long enough for a real man to seek me out. Instead, many years went by before I'd realized that expecting to get my true happiness from someone else was all a waste of time and energy. It had been within me all along. Discovering this was devastating. I may not have known myself back then, but I certainly do now because no one is ever beyond repair, not even me.